TO BE AN AGNOSTIC

An Agnostic Approach to Life, Liberty,
and the Pursuit of Happiness

James Kirk Wall

iUniverse, Inc.
New York   Bloomington

To Be an Agnostic
An Agnostic Approach to Life, Liberty, and the Pursuit of Happiness

iUniverse books may be ordered through booksellers or by contacting:

iUniverse
1663 Liberty Drive
Bloomington, IN 47403
www.iuniverse.com
1-800-Authors (1-800-288-4677)

Because of the dynamic nature of the Internet, any Web addresses or links contained in this book may have changed since publication and may no longer be valid. The views expressed in this work are solely those of the author and do not necessarily reflect the views of the publisher, and the publisher hereby disclaims any responsibility for them.

ISBN: 978-1-4401-6658-7 (pbk)
ISBN: 978-1-4401-6656-3 (cloth)
ISBN: 978-1-4401-6657-0 (ebook)

Printed in the United States of America

iUniverse rev. date: 8/12/09

CONTENTS

ACKNOWLEDGMENTS

I would like to thank all the great teachers, philosophers, historians, epistemologists, psychologists, neurologists, anatomists, sociologists, archeologists, biologists, microbiologists, zoologists, physicists, astronomers, chemists, geologists, economists, religious leaders, non-religious leaders, political leaders and other great people of knowledge past and present for their contribution to education. I would like to thank the College of DuPage and the University of Phoenix.

Much of my knowledge has come from self-study. I would like to thank a wonderful organization called The Teaching Company for making my countless driving trips to remote clients meaningful and enjoyable. This establishment promotes lifelong learning through audio courses. The Teaching Company courses I have enjoyed include the following which are listed by title and professor:

History of Ancient Egypt – Bob Brier
Ancient Greek Civilization – Jeremy McInerney
Alexander the Great and the Hellenistic Age – Jeremy McInerney
Famous Greeks – J. Rufus Fears
From Yao to Mao 5000 Years of Chinese History – Kenneth J. Hammond
Greek Tragedy – Elizabeth Vandiver
History of Science Antiquity to 1700 – Lawrence M. Principe
Human Prehistory and the First Civilizations – Brian M. Fagan
Neolithic Europe - Jeremy Adams
Old Testament – Amy-Jill Levine

The Discovery of Ancient Civilizations - Brian Fagan
The History of Ancient Rome – Garrett G. Fagan
Thomas Jefferson American Visionary - Darren Staloff
Plato, Socrates and the Dialogues – Michael Sugrue
World Philosophy - Kathleen Higgins
Historical Jesus – Bart D. Ehrman

Another company that provides audio learning is the Barnes & Noble Portable Professor series. The Portable Professor courses I have enjoyed include the following which I will list by title and professor:

Everything You've Been Taught Is Wrong – James W. Loewen
Eternal Questions, Timeless Approaches – Colin McGinn
What Would Socrates Do? – Peter Kreeft
Evolution and Its Discontents – Chandak Sengoopta
Questions of Faith – Peter Kreeft

Special thanks to my wife Pamela of twenty years for teaching me not to be too rational and that emotions and feeling are important. Thanks to my son Scott for teaching me patience and perseverance.

PREFACE

Socrates (469-399 B.C.) was the wisest man in Athens Greece during his time and one of the greatest philosophers in the world of all time. Ironically he was not wise because of what he knew but rather because of what he didn't know. The difference was Socrates acknowledged what he didn't know while proclaimed wise men did not.

Socrates had a reputation for scrutinizing what were considered to be known facts such as the understanding of justice, and making well respected bureaucrats appear bumbling and ignorant. Socrates was fearless in challenging the knowledge and wisdom of powerful men and the immorality of the ancient Greek Gods, which was his country's religion during his time.

How well would our truths hold up to Socrates' scrutiny in cross examination? How often are people forced to defend their beliefs or opinions? Don't talk about religion and politics right? Let's make sure all our relationships are superficial, where we don't challenge opinions or so called foundations of knowledge or belief. Heaven forbid we force people to think, and take their hypotheses to the next level, or challenge the status quo.

So what does this have to do with being an agnostic? To be agnostic is to be without knowledge. To be without knowledge means knowledge needs to be obtained. To be an agnostic is to be a philosopher. Philosophy is the love of knowledge and wisdom. Acquiring true knowledge requires impeccable research and thinking, or philosophizing.

This book is about knowledge and wisdom. I'm going to explore what we know, and what we don't know. There are countless instances where the absolute truth is unknown and therefore, theories are required. We need theories; however, they need to be recognized for what they are.

My objective of writing this book is to promote added perspective and open mindedness. This is not a book about attacking beliefs. It's a book about critical thinking and free thinking. The greatest questions of our existence will be tackled with perspective from various sources, sciences and other academic studies. Be prepared to be challenged and to expand your mind to new definitions and views. Furthermore, be prepared to have fun. This is not some stuffy high brow scholarly manuscript written by a Doctor of Philosophy for other Doctors of Philosophy. Simplicity is the essence of truth and most of this book merely states the obvious.

WHAT IS AN AGNOSTIC?

"Deep doubts, deep wisdom; small doubts, little wisdom." – Chinese Proverb

I'm about to ruin the definition of agnostic that you may be used to. To be an agnostic is to be a free thinker who challenges authority, and doesn't limit sources of knowledge and wisdom. If one was to research agnosticism, one would find various definitions and thousands of ways to slice and dice this belief. The true definition is quite simple, and it's time to remove the clouds of confusion. An agnostic believes when knowledge is lacking for an absolute conclusion to a question or problem, a neutral and factual approach is the right method for obtaining truth. Additional effort is required to find the answer, or solidify the one that we have. This term is typically tied to religious beliefs, but can be used in any situation that requires further thought.

I have been an agnostic my entire life, which means I have always possessed an agnostic view of religion. My parents were Christians; however, I was simply never inspired by the Bible or Christian teachers to be one myself. While Christians read the Bible as the words inspired by God, I read the Bible as stories and myths written by various men. I'm a philosopher who deeply contemplates life, death, the universe and everything. I have spent countless hours obsessing, studying and philosophizing about the greatest questions of our existence. I don't believe in limiting sources of knowledge to specific people or faiths; the broader the spectrum of knowledge the better.

In order to further define the meaning of agnosticism, we should first discuss the agnostic approach. This term is gaining popularity as a method for making sound business decisions. In a nutshell, the agnostic approach is an inquisitive neutral approach. There is no formal definition of this method; the following is my own professional opinion. The agnostic approach is to take the following method when faced with a situation that requires judgment or action:

- *Begin with uncertainty and doubt, question everything*
- *Take a non-biased neutral approach*
- *Look at the situation from all angles*
- *Gather and validate the facts*
- *Make an informed decision*

Begin with uncertainty and doubt, question everything – take nothing for granted. Don't accept "because that's the way we've always done it" or "everybody is doing it that way" as a valid reason to do anything without further research.

Take a non-biased neutral approach – We are all biased. It's important that we recognize and are aware of our biases and work to maintain a neutral approach. This means we must clear our minds and start with a fresh perspective. Jumping to conclusions based on prejudice is not an agnostic approach. Rushing to judgment based on mob mentality is not an agnostic approach.

Look at the situation from all angles – This takes thought and imagination. This includes putting yourself in someone else's shoes. Expanding the view also means expanding the sources of knowledge. The more angles we use to view a situation the more holistic the view becomes. For example, let's analyze a small white pebble by the single sense of touch. The pebble is small, smooth, cool and hard. Opening the floodgate of senses and angles we expand the identified characteristics of this pebble to include: small, smooth, cool, hard, white, scentless, quiet, tasteless, rock, stone, non-edible, sinks, light, reflective, solid, non-porous, throw-able, non-organic, mineral, old, water-resistant, abundant, worthless, useless, circular, rounded, lifeless, classless, sexless, pattern-less, eroded, strong, non-transparent, non-metallic, dull, pearly, egg-like, etc.

If this many attributes can be identified for something as simple as a lifeless pebble, imagine listing all the attributes for every part and the whole of a plant or insect. Imagine listing all the attributes for every part and the whole of a human. If one explores all the attributes of a human, one will recognize features such as skin color are extremely minute parts of the equation. It's important to look at a situation from all angles as we often jump to the wrong conclusions by not getting the whole story or picture.

Gather and validate the facts – Do we automatically assume something is true because someone says it is or writes it down?

"Owners of capital will stimulate the working class to buy more and more expensive goods, houses and technology, pushing them to take more and more expensive credits, until their debt becomes unbearable. The unpaid debt will lead to bankruptcy of banks, which will have to be nationalized and the State will have to take the road which will eventually lead to Communism."
- Karl Marx, Das Kapital 1867

This would be quite a sobering and ominous story if it were true. After this story was e-mailed to me by a friend, I did some investigation and found this story is actually fiction.

Have you ever reacted strongly to some piece of information only to find out later it was an intentionally or accidentally false statement or claim? When there is a claim, are there facts behind the claim? If there are facts, what are the facts? Are the facts solid, or have they been distorted by bias, misunderstanding or someone or some groups political or financial agenda? If someone is performing research and the financial security of his or her own family is determined by one outcome over another, they are likely to find a way to conclude the theory that provides the financial benefit is true.

Would you believe taste test results from a cola company? If the competitor's drink is served warm and flat while the sponsor's drink is served fresh and ice cold, how much is the test result worth? The answer of course is nothing. Facts must be gathered carefully. Do your research and identify trusted sources of knowledge. When one uses an effective method and trusted sources for the obtainment of knowledge, they become a trusted source of knowledge for others.

Make an informed decision – Don't be a sheep. Due diligence will lead to informed decisions. Informed decisions lead to better decisions and better results.

"Doubt is the key to knowledge." – Persian Proverb

Don't let partners and vendors dictate your business decisions and processes; let your business decisions and processes dictate your partners and vendors. Take a partner neutral and vendor neutral approach to make the best decisions for your company. Businesses must exist in a constant state or re-evaluation in order to keep up with change. This would be an agnostic approach.

Who is the greatest sports figure of all time? When asked that question one is likely to think of their own favorite sports figure or popular athlete during his or her own generation. We are naturally biased. In order to come up with a well researched rational answer one needs to look at the facts and have a definition of greatest. Socrates taught knowledge begins by properly defining terms.

If greatest is defined as most popular then perhaps we would need facts regarding number of attendees at stadiums multiplied by number of appearances and popular opinion. Perhaps we could investigate stadium attendance, television ratings and internet searches to make a solid conclusion. Number of internet searches has become a widely used method for measuring popularity. If we chose a modern research method such as number of internet searches, then all sports figures from previous generations may be ruled out as they are not popular now, or at the time these internet searches began to be recorded. Greatest is a very broad term.

Let's narrow it down to greatest basketball player of all time. Once again, we need a definition of greatest. Does the term greatest mean highest scorer, rebounder, athletic ability, highest shooting percentage, most popular, center, point guard, 3-point shooter, etc? Who's the greatest scorer of all time? At the time of this writing the answer is Kareem Abdul-Jabbar if we evaluate the criteria by the most total points scored (38,387 career points, nba.com). If the criterion is points per game, then Kareem is not the greatest. If we use the most points scored as the criterion, some will argue it's not a fair statistic as the rules have changed that would make the past feat by Kareem much more challenging now. Can we get a decisive answer? In this instance we cannot as the question is loosely defined, and there are too many factors. We can merely express opinion. With due diligence, we can express an educated opinion backed up by facts rather than an uninformed opinion which means next to nothing.

At one time or another everyone has used an agnostic approach to solve a problem. When it comes to religious beliefs such as answering the question, "what religion are you?" using an agnostic approach in itself does not make someone an agnostic. One can be a Christian in religion but when it comes to certain non-religious matters be an agnostic. Being an agnostic when it comes to religion is taking the agnostic approach towards religion. The purpose of an agnostic approach is to provide a framework for well informed decisions. When it comes to absolute truth in religion, the great agnostic conclusion is we simply don't know as knowledge is lacking to provide an absolute conclusion. An agnostic in the religious sense does not believe in the divinity of any organized religion nor does an agnostic deny the existence of a greater being or God(s).

Agnostic literally means without knowledge. It comes from the Greek language; the prefix "a" meaning without and Gnostic meaning knowledge. The term agnostic was first published in 1870 and coined by British scientist Thomas H. Huxley (1825 – 1895). So who was the man who created the term?

The following quotes by Thomas Huxley tell us much about who he was and his philosophy:

1. *"Every great advance in natural knowledge has involved the absolute rejection of authority."*
2. *"Freedom and order are not incompatible... truth is strength... free discussion is the very life of truth."*
3. *"I took thought, and invented what I conceived to be the appropriate title of 'agnostic'."*
4. *"Irrationally held truths may be more harmful than reasoned errors."*

5. *"It is not to be forgotten that what we call rational grounds for our beliefs are often extremely irrational attempts to justify our instincts."*

6. *"It is not who is right, but what is right, that is of importance."*

7. *"Learn what is true in order to do what is right."*

8. *"Logical consequences are the scarecrows of fools and the beacons of wise men."*

9. *"My business is to teach my aspirations to confirm themselves to fact, not to try and make facts harmonize with my aspirations."*

10. *"Nothing can be more incorrect than the assumption one sometimes meets with, that physics has one method, chemistry another, and biology a third."*

11. *"Science is organized common sense where many a beautiful theory was killed by an ugly fact."*

12. *"Science has fulfilled her function when she has ascertained and enunciated truth."*

13. *"Sit down before fact as a little child, be prepared to give up every conceived notion, follow humbly wherever and whatever abysses nature leads, or you will learn nothing."*

14. *"Teach a child what is wise, that is morality. Teach him what is wise and beautiful, that is religion!"*

15. *"The chess-board is the world, the pieces are the phenomena of the universe, the rules of the game are what we call the laws of Nature. The player on the other side is hidden from us."*

16. *"The improver of natural knowledge absolutely refuses to acknowledge authority, as such. For him, skepticism is the highest of duties; blind faith the one unpardonable sin."*

17. *"The man of science has learned to believe in justification, not by faith, but by verification."*

18. *"The most considerable difference I note among men is not in their readiness to fall into error, but in their readiness to acknowledge these inevitable lapses."*

19. *"The ultimate court of appeal is observation and experiment... not authority."*

20. *"Time, whose tooth gnaws away everything else, is powerless against truth."*

At the time of this writing a common synonym for agnostic is doubter. This is an extremely poor translation. A better synonym for agnostic is neutral. To be without knowledge is to be neutral until such knowledge is obtained to take one side over the other. An agnostic should not be confused with an atheist who denies the existence of a supreme being. A skeptic has similarities to an agnostic in that a skeptic questions beliefs and so called truths. The difference is a skeptic has a doubting nature and questions any validity of truth. An agnostic is far more open-minded.

The terms atheist and skeptic have been around much longer than the term agnostic. Thomas Huxley was a highly educated man and a scientist. He created the term agnostic because no other term during his time accurately reflected his view of religion. If the term atheist matched his beliefs then Mr. Huxley would have merely declared himself an atheist. Agnostic has a completely different meaning than atheist. If the term skeptic matched his beliefs then Mr. Huxley would have merely declared himself a skeptic. Agnostic has a completely different meaning than skeptic and Thomas Huxley was hardly someone who thought truth could never be obtained. He was an outspoken man who strongly defended science and research, especially that of his close friend Charles Darwin, who is famous for his theories of evolution.

Some have gone through great lengths to create multiple erroneous and absurd definitions of agnostic and atheist. At some time, someone created an additional definition of atheist to mean perhaps there is a God rather than the primary definition of, there is no God. This is akin to creating one term that means capitalism but has an alternate definition that means communism. The notion that one term would have multiple definitions with such an extreme difference in philosophy is absurd and confusing. Perhaps this was done unintentionally by someone who was perchance thinking too much or intentionally to confuse and weaken the terms and alternate views to organized religion. These terms are not complex, they are very simple. For the purposes of this book, I will state the primary definitions of the three mentioned terms to clearly demonstrate the differences and remove the confusion often caused by over analysis:

Belief	Is there a God(s)?
Atheist	No
Skeptic	We don't know and never will.
Agnostic	There is currently not sufficient evidence to prove the divinity of any religious doctrine. The truth regarding God is yet to be discovered if it is to be discovered.

WHO WAS SOCRATES AND WHY DO WE CARE?

"Well I am certainly wiser than this man. It is only too likely that neither of us has any knowledge to boast of; but he thinks that he knows something which he does not know, whereas I am quite conscious of my ignorance. At any rate it seems that I am wiser than he is to this small extent, that I do not think that I know what I do not know."   – Socrates (469-399 B.C.)

Socrates is to agnosticism as Jesus Christ is to Christianity. Socrates acknowledged that he knew nothing. The definition of agnostic is without knowledge. To be an agnostic is to have an exact match to the primary principles of philosophy as Socrates, who is one of the most influential figures in Western civilization. Socrates has a scholarly lineage that extends to Cleopatra, the last pharaoh of Egypt, and the academic and democratic government structures of modern society. Not a bad accomplishment for a poor stone cutter of small stature.

Humanists claim Socrates as one of their own. Is that true? What is a humanist?

- Religious – God made man in the image of God.
- Humanist – man made God in the image of man.

Humanists focus on the capacity and potential of the human race in terms of high moral ethics and worth regardless of supernatural beliefs. Humanists argue that mankind is more than capable of morality with or without religion.

Socrates was a pious man who preached virtues, morality and ethics. In the spirit of Socrates, these terms will be defined as that's where knowledge begins. Unlike Socrates the definitions will be short and without further scrutiny.

- *Pious and piety* – Faithful, devoted, dutiful and committed to goodness
- *Virtuous* – In accordance with principles of the highest conduct and moral excellence
- *Morality* – A system of ideas of right and wrong
- *Ethics* – A moral obligation to do the best for mankind

Socrates taught self examination, wisdom and ethics, but was he a humanist? He questioned his people's religion but was passionate about following the Athenian religious customs. Athens Greece during Socrates' time worshiped the Greek Gods. Greek mythology is an extensive and complex story book of Gods, Goddesses, mythical creatures and heroes. Greek mythology was not about ethics; in fact, many of the Gods including the mighty Zeus were unethical in their actions. In one story Zeus seduces a mortal woman Alcmene while disguised as her husband Amphitryon. Zeus was so inflamed with lust and passion while in bed with Amphitryon that he altered time to extend one night into three. Not exactly the good moral compass for society one would expect from the mightiest God. The Greek Gods were about love, compassion, hate, power, lust, jealousy, spite and revenge. There is also wisdom in the ancient writings that must have influenced Socrates to some extent.

The Olympian Greek Gods and Goddesses included:

- *Zeus* – The heavenly King of the Gods and ruler of mankind
- *Apollo* – The youthful God of the Sun and the Music
- *Aphrodite* – The sensual Goddess of Beauty
- *Hades* – The gloomy God of the Underworld
- *Poseidon* – The moody God of the Seas
- *Athena* – The sophisticated goddess of Wisdom and Arts

- *Hera* – The mature Goddess of the Family
- *Dionysus* – The joyful God of the Wine
- *Ares* – The bloodthirsty God of War
- *Artemis* – The wild Goddess of the Hunt
- *Demeter* – The natural Goddess of the Harvest
- *Hephaestus* – The ill-favored God of Metallurgy
- *Hermes* – The cunning God of the Trade
- *Hestia* – The calm Goddess of the Hearth

(Greek-Gods.Info, Gods & Goddesses of Ancient Greece, www.greek-gods.info/greek-gods)

Despite irresolvable differences with the morality and ethics of the Greek Gods, Socrates was not an atheist. He believed in a soul and even redefined the meaning. During his time, the soul was simply a shadowy version of the self. Socrates redefined the soul as containing our morality and our wisdom. Not a shadowy version but rather something greater than our physical bodies. He also clearly had high regard for the Delphic Oracle (a priestess of the Greek God Apollo, who is legend to have spoken under the God's inspiration). "Know thyself" was taught by Socrates but has Greek mythological origins and was carved into the temple of Apollo: GNOTHI SEAUTON, Know thyself.

This wisdom was later carried on by Muhammad, "Learn to know thyself." – Prophet Muhammad (570-632)

The Oracle Delphic Sibyl by Michelangelo

11

Socrates' friend Chaerephon asked the Delphic Oracle if Socrates was the wisest man in Athens. The Oracle told Chaerephon that he was indeed. When Socrates learned this, he didn't believe it. He embarked on a quest to find someone in Athens wiser than he. Socrates never found anyone wiser. What he found were people who professed knowledge but had none. He developed the Socratic Method of cross examination for finding the truth.

Socrates had a young following. Why was this? In order to have a young following does not one need to be cool? The Greeks knew all about physical completion through the Olympics. What Socrates brought was mental competition through his own Socratic Method. Imagine being with Socrates as some arrogant snobby aristocrat comes walking by. Socrates fearlessly engages the gentleman in rhetoric asking simple questions at first but eventually giving him an intellectual thrashing and sending him off looking like a fool. I'm sure we all know people we'd like to see get knocked off their high horse. This must have been highly entertaining but did make Socrates many enemies.

So what were Socrates' religious beliefs? He believed in a soul but didn't believe it was a shadowy version of the self that would go to Hades. The spirituality of Socrates can be found in his following quotes:

- "The end of life is to be like God, and the soul following God will be like him."
- "I pray thee, O God, that I may be beautiful within."
- "The fewer our wants the more we resemble the Gods."

The following is the quote of Socrates when sentenced to death that cements him as an agnostic, although a theist (one who believes in a God) agnostic. "The hour of departure has arrived and we go our ways; I to die, and you to live. Which is better? Only God knows."

There are some similarities in the life and death of Socrates and that of Jesus Christ. Both men did not write their own teachings and both preached a tolerance for enemies. Both were unjustly sentenced to death. Plato was the most famous student of Socrates and wrote about his life. Socrates inspired Plato to give up writing Greek tragedies and devote his life to philosophy. Plato was a gifted writer who immortalized his teacher in his works Apology, Republic, Crito and Phaedo. Although other historical information about Socrates can be found in Alcibiades's speech in the Symposium and Xenophon's Mernorabilia, if it were not for Plato, we would not be discussing Socrates over 2,300 years after his life.

Without Plato, there is no Socrates and without Socrates, there is very likely no Plato in modern thoughts and discussions. Without the disciples, there is no Jesus just as without Jesus, there are no disciples in modern times. Oral tradition only goes so far, in order for teachings to last good writing is required. We don't know which of Plato's writings about Socrates are completely accurate as Plato uses him as a heroic character in many of his works about political ethics. The same can be said about the disciples writing of Jesus as there are some contradictions between earlier and later writings. We do get a clear essence of each historical figure.

Plato (427-347 B.C.) had an enormous impact on Western philosophy. His most popular work is The Republic. While Socrates' teachings promoted self evaluation and improvement, Plato focused on politics and society. Plato argued that the best government was ruled by philosophers. He coined the phrase philosopher king. In 387 B.C. Plato founded the first institutional school of philosophy named the Academy in Athens, Greece. This advanced educational institution of philosophical and scientific discussion stood for approx. 1,000 years until the 6th century when it was closed by Christian emperor Justinian.

We have Plato from Socrates, and now it's time to discuss Aristotle, who was a student of Plato and another great philosopher. He was also a scientist with tremendous influence on modern society. Aristotle (384-322 B.C.) continued in his predecessors' footsteps in regard to teaching ethics, but also expanded into scientific observation about the natural and physical world. He set the stage for the modern study of biology. His works included physics, metaphysics, rhetoric and ethics. Aristotle founded another educational institution known as the Lyceum. Of the "great three" as these philosophers are referred as Aristotle was much more of a scientist than Socrates or Plato. His works are vast as he seemingly tries to answer all questions in life. He greatly advanced science during his time and beyond.

Aristotle's surviving works on science and philosophy include

Eudemus (On the Soul), On Philosophy, On Monarchy, On Justice, On the Poets, On Wealth, On Prayer, On Good Birth, On Pleasure, On Education, Constitution of the Athenians, On Heaven, On Generation and Corruption, Meteorology, On the Soul, History of Animals, On the Origin of Animals, Nicornachean Ethics, Politics, Poetics, On Interpretation, On the Movement of Animals, On Feeling and the Senses, On Memory and Recollection, On Dreams, On Life and Death and On Breathing. One thing is for certain, Aristotle was not lazy.

Aristotle had a student who just happened to be the Macedonian conqueror of the ancient world. Alexander the Great (356-323 B.C.) defeated the mighty Persian army and nearly conquered the entire civilized world. For three years Aristotle taught Alexander philosophy, government, politics, poetry, drama and the sciences.

The Greek empire stretched from the edge of western modern day India across Egypt under Alexander's military conquest. In Egypt, he founded the city of Alexandria, which became a famous prosperous city rich in culture and knowledge. There was influence of Aristotle on Alexander. Alexander was more than a military brute. He was cultured and respected the local customs and religions in the lands he defeated. In Egypt, he was declared a pharaoh. The oracle of the Egyptian God Amun translated in Greek to Ammon greeted Alexander as the son of Ammon. To be a pharaoh in ancient Egypt was more than to be an emperor or king. To be a pharaoh was to be a God among men.

Although cultured and respectful of ancient traditions in other lands, the conquests of Alexander were brutal and his military strategies were later adopted and perfected by the Romans. Ultimately, this military campaign did not advance moral principles in the spirit of Socrates and Plato but rather resulted in a Greek rule that would be broken by internal conflict and the rise of the oppressive Roman Empire. To magnify the lack of ethics and reverence during this time, Alexander's own wife and son were assassinated after his own death. His young son was perceived as a threat to those in power, and those in power had him murdered.

Alexander died in 323 B.C. at 32 years of age from malaria. The empire was divided among his four top generals. One general was Ptolemy, who took control of Egypt. By all accounts Ptolemy was a good man with high regard for his fallen leader. Ptolemy through force took the body of Alexander and placed his tomb in the city Alexandria in Egypt. Alexandria became Egypt's capitol and was later famous for the Lighthouse of Alexandria, which is one of the Seven Wonders of the ancient world and for the Library of Alexandria, which was the largest library in the ancient world. Ptolemy was declared pharaoh of Egypt and his blood line ruled Egypt for 300 years. Cleopatra was the last Egyptian pharaoh and Ptolemy to rule Egypt. The three thousand year reign of Egyptian pharaohs and all the ancient Egyptian Gods fell with Roman occupation.

The ancient Greeks were influenced by and revered the ancient Egyptians. They often traveled to Egypt for wisdom and answers to problems such as how Olympic competition for foreign athletes could be fairly refereed and judged. The Romans were influenced by the Greeks, especially Alexander the Great. The Romans spoke both Latin and the Greek language. The New Testament has Greek influence. The Bible was written in both Hebrew and Greek. How much if any of Jesus' ethical teachings were influenced by Socrates? It's hard to say for certain.

Have you ever wondered how education and science evolved to what it is now, why our government is constructed the way it is, why our justice system is the way it is, why we think about democracy the way we do? Much of this is attributed to the ancient Greeks.

- "The people have a right to the truth as they have a right to life, liberty and the pursuit of happiness." – Epictetus (50-120)
- "We hold these truths to be self-evident, that all men are created equal, that they are endowed by their Creator with certain unalienable Rights, that among these are Life, Liberty and the pursuit of Happiness." – United States Declaration of Independence (July 4, 1776)

What does this have to do with being an agnostic? By knowing our history and studying various sources of knowledge, we can better obtain the truth. Socrates' admission of ignorance, challenging of authority, and relentless quest for knowledge makes him an agnostic. Socrates was a moral and ethical free thinker who broke through political and religious barriers to elevate and redefine knowledge and wisdom.

"True wisdom comes to each of us when we realize how little we understand about life, ourselves, and the world around us."

- Socrates

EDUCATION AND ARGUMENTATION

"Try to learn something about everything and everything about
something."   -- Thomas H. Huxley (1825 – 1895)

To be an agnostic is to begin without knowledge and then build
understanding upon a solid and level foundation. The goal of an
agnostic is to obtain knowledge and thereby obtain truth. We don't
give up on knowledge; we go out and get it to the best of our ability.
We need to become educated. The more subjects we are educated in
the more holistic our life view becomes. Obviously, we don't have the
capacity to be intimate with every bit of knowledge over the past many
millenniums. We also don't want to be a jack of all trades and master
of none.

As Mr. Huxley eloquently states in the opening quote, we should
go broad and shallow overall and then deep in certain areas when it
comes to the obtainment of knowledge. There are so many instances
where truths share common ground among different subjects, religions
and philosophies. There are also many instances where wisdom binds
together between the past and present times. Without a broad range of
knowledge, we lack the perspective necessary to identify and connect
multiple instances of truth from various sources. Education is the
difference between a two-dimensional and three-dimensional view of
the world.

> "Our progress as a nation can be no swifter than our progress in education. The human mind is our fundamental resource."
> – John F. Kennedy (1917-1963)

Education and wealth are the largest dividers of class in society, and they are directly related. Taking an agnostic approach means finding and validating facts. In this world of misinformation validating facts can be difficult. Being educated is a key part of finding truth. Knowing the art of argumentation is also key as not only is it important to make informed decisions, but also to articulate and drive informed decisions. The best product in the world will fail without effective marketing and sales. A liar with good political skills will win arguments over people who know the truth, but are unable to articulate it.

In the preface, I stated this book is about knowledge, free thinking and critical thinking. Although the subject can be monotonous and somewhat overly logical, critical thinking is a key life skill to have as it allows for a formal structured approach to problem solving. If you have not learned about this subject through a course in an educational institution, please spend some time in self-study to gain more knowledge. What is critical thinking?

Definition

"Critical thinking is that mode of thinking - about any subject, content, or problem - in which the thinker improves the quality of his or her thinking by skillfully taking charge of the structures inherent in thinking and imposing intellectual standards upon them.

The Result

A well cultivated critical thinker: raises vital questions and problems, formulating them clearly and precisely; gathers and assesses relevant information, using abstract ideas to interpret it effectively comes to well-reasoned conclusions and solutions, testing them against relevant criteria and standards; thinks open-mindedly within alternative systems of thought, recognizing and assessing, as need be, their assumptions, implications, and practical consequences; and communicates effectively with others in figuring out solutions to complex problems." (CriticalThinking.org)

What is education? The obtainment of a college degree is a means to get educated but by far not the only means. Education is simply acquiring knowledge. In fact, most education happens outside of school in our lives and on the job. Anybody who's good at anything is educated. An athlete is educated in exercise and nutrition. Sports commentators are educated in broadcasting and sports. Police officers are educated in law and law enforcement. Criminals such as drug dealers are educated in committing crime. There are people who don't have degrees but are highly self-educated and those who have street smarts. I believe in life learning. Regardless of the attainment of any educational degree acquiring knowledge should never stop.

> "Seek knowledge from the cradle to the grave."
> – Prophet Muhammad (570-632)

What are the benefits of education? I will provide an example that deals with law. We live in a society of law. Laws do not enforce themselves, people enforce laws. People cannot enforce laws if they don't know what the laws are. People cannot defend their rights if they don't know what their rights are. Political corruption will go unchecked if no one realizes it is taking place. We must be educated in what we do to make a living. We also must be educated to know what our rights are and how our political system works, to protect ourselves and each other. This does not mean everyone needs to have a degree in law. It only means we should at least know the basics. We should at least be familiar with the main points and have a means of acquiring greater knowledge when necessary.

- "I love argument, I love debate. I don't expect anyone just sit there and agree with me, that's not their job." – Margaret Thatcher

If everyone in authoritative positions had the same attitude of argumentation as Margaret Thatcher, the world would be a better place. Someone who is secure in themselves and secure in their beliefs should not avoid or fear a healthy debate. What is argumentation?

Argumentation should not be perceived as something bad. It's merely a debate with different points of view. Argumentation provides excellent benefits when it is done respectfully. Through discussions, we can obtain different and unique outlooks on particular issues. This enables us to obtain a more holistic view through diversity by gathering different perspectives.

If one was to perform a self analysis through completing a questionnaire, he or she would understand themselves through their own perspective. If this questionnaire was also completed by friends and coworkers to assess him or her, then that person would also obtain the perspective of themselves from other people. How do you perceive yourself? How are you perceived by others? Do the perceptions match?

Be prepared to defend your beliefs. Arm yourself for battle. This does not mean winning at all costs because sometimes it's best to back off an argument in order to regroup. This also does not mean never admitting you're wrong if someone presents a case that clearly proves your argument doesn't hold up. Sometimes arguing is not worth the fight as winning the argument may lead to alienating people rather than uniting them. One needs to make judgments based on political realities. It would be great to be fearless like Socrates, but it's also nice to keep a job and a paycheck. Often battles need to be picked carefully.

Being prepared for an argument includes anticipation of objections and counter arguments. In 1984 Ronald Reagan prepared for a presidential debate with Walter Mondale. At 73 years of age, Reagan and his advisors knew the subject of being old would come up as an attack ploy by his opponent. When it did, Ronald Reagan countered by promising not to exploit for political purposes his opponent's youth and inexperience. The counter attack was humorous and at the same time extremely successful.

> "When I'm getting ready to reason with a man, I spend one-third of my time thinking about myself and what I am going to say and two-thirds thinking about him and what he is going to say."
> – Abraham Lincoln (1809-1865)

I would encourage anyone and everyone to spend some time reading The *Art of War* by Sun Tzu written in the 6th century B.C. The English translation by Lionel Giles is easy to read, concise, and pure genius. This translation is also freely available on the web at the time of this writing. (Sun Tzu on the Art of War the Oldest Military Treatise in the World, www.chinapage.com/sunzi-e.html). Through this content one will learn ancient military tactics that apply to business management, including argumentation and negotiation. Sun Tzu teaches not to besiege walled cities and to convert defeated enemies to your own side rather than destroy them. The following quote is in regard to deception.

"18. All warfare is based on deception.

19. Hence, when able to attack, we must seem unable; when using our forces, we must seem inactive; when we are near, we must make the enemy believe we are far away; when far away, we must make him believe we are near."

(Sun Tzu - The Art of War)

I would never condone using deception or other nefarious means in argumentation. Integrity and reputation are to be maintained; however, be wary of your opponent and understand deceptive tactics may be used against you.

Now it's time to explore fallacious arguments. It's important to be familiar with these techniques as it will help you know when someone might be misleading you.

- "The jawbone of an ass is just as dangerous a weapon today as in Sampson's time." -- Richard Nixon (1913-1994)
- "The trouble with the world is not that people know too little, but that they know so many things that ain't so." – Mark Twain (1835-1910)

Fallacious augments include:

1. *Ad Hominem* – Attack on the presenter rather than addressing the argument. For example – You eat meat! No one cares what you have to say about animal abuse you meat eater!

2. *Needling* – Not addressing the argument but attempting to make the other person angry by being obnoxious or disrespect-ful. This is an important one to be aware of in today's media world of mass communication and shock jocks. If someone loses their cool and has an outburst over obnoxious or disre-spectful treatment it can be turned into a repeated sound or

video bite on national television and popular web sites thereby making the person receiving the disrespect appear foolish regardless of any legitimacy to the outburst.

3. *Straw Man* – Exaggerating the opponent's position. For example – By advocating gay marriage, my opponent is also advocating polygamy.

4. *Inflation of Conflict* – insinuating conflict between scholars is larger than it really is. This is an important one to be aware of as there will always be differences of opinions among people of academic accreditation. If someone states there is disagreement within the scientific community, what exactly does that mean? Does it mean one scientist out of five-hundred disagrees?

5. *Argument from Adverse Consequences* – Either opponent is wrong or bad things will happen. For example – If my opponent is right, it will be the end of the world as we know it.

6. *Excluded Middle* – Claiming there are only two alternatives when there are many. For example – The only alternative to Christianity is atheism.

7. *Argument from False Authority* – For example – all superintendents we interviewed agreed our product increased lung capacity.

8. *Appeal to Anonymous Authority* – For example – Some experts agree our value could skyrocket in the next few months.

9. *Bad Analogy* – comparing two situations that are not similar. For example – My father was an alcoholic, so I'm going to be an alcoholic.

10. *False Cause* – Claiming when two events occurred, that one caused the second. For example – Ever since they changed stadiums, that team has never been to the finals. Was changing stadiums the real reason for not making the finals?

11. *Appeal to Widespread Belief* – Claim is true because many believe it. For example – Everyone knows politicians lie and my opponent is a politician.

12. *Complex Question* – One question combining points, as if they should be accepted together. For example – Don't you believe in astrology and science?

13. *Slippery Slope Fallacy* – Claiming something is wrong and will slide towards other wrongs. For example – Once we legalize gay marriage the next thing you know we'll have legalized polygamy and marriages between people and farm animals.
14. *Argument by Pigheadedness* – refusing to accept generally established facts. For example – I don't care what you say; the Earth is the center of the universe.
15. *Argument by Repetition* – keep repeating arguments until people believe it. This is an important one to be mindful of. When using an internet search engine, there may be pages of biased results from a search that come up due to an organization with an agenda. They intentionally post a torrent of articles that have the same biased point of view to try and drown out any opposing position. For example – do a search for "How old is the earth?" How many results are for the young earth theory vs. the established old earth theory?
16. *Argument by Half Truth* – This is deceptive argumentation where the presenter counts on the participants not asking questions or performing research. For example – "The analysts downgraded the stock to sell. The stock price fell over 50%." Both sentences are correct; however, how would you feel about the analysts' competence if you found out the stock fell over 50% and then the analysts downgraded the stock?
17. *Argument by Selective Observation* – Highlighting only the positive aspects. For example – Casinos are great for the community because they create jobs and give away millions of dollars. This statement does not address how many people lose money gambling.
18. *Argument by Generalization* – promotes a conclusion based on a small unrelated sample. For example – We shouldn't pay taxes because our state senator is a known tax cheat.
19. *Argument by Gibberish* – making up argument responses in order to confuse people and change the focus rather than addressing the real argument. This technique if often used by people who are losing an argument. For example – I can legally deny employee bonuses because as a state legal representative I have the right to protect based on the constitutional amendment

which focuses on the equal protection wage earning rights the unequal misrepresentation of a company's harmful compensation practices against the people's right of equal pay.

20. *Argumentation by Lies* – intentional misrepresentation of facts. For example – America is more of a terrorist organization than Al-Qaida. Although despicable and not used by anyone with integrity, lying can be an effective argumentation technique. It can throw the opposition off balance, and contesting the lie can unintentionally give the lie substance and completely derail the original argument.

21. *Argumentation through Changing the Subject* – This technique is often used as a desperation tactic by those who are losing the original argument. For example – You argue against pollution but your candidate has four big gas guzzlers. Why does he have so many trucks?

(A List of Fallacious Arguments, http://www.don-lindsay-archive.org/skeptic/arguments.html)

There is also the likability factor in argumentation as there is in politics. When people like someone, they are more likely to follow their lead, and less likely to negatively criticize. When people do not like someone, they will be watching for any misstep or gaffe and ready to pounce. Political groups through the media, can raise with praise someone's popularity, or destroy someone's credibility with personal attacks.

I'm by no means a fan of former vice president Dan Quayle; however, I will never forget when a mob turned against him and labeled him an idiot for misspelling the word potato. If the definition of an idiot is one who misspells a word, then all of us are idiots. Before instinctively joining in on any worshiping or witch hunts, one should gain some neutral perspective and get the facts.

There are many sources to increase knowledge and improve argumentation skills. It's important to note the agnostic approach promotes informed decisions, not popular decisions. Be prepared to defend your beliefs, and fight for truth.

Many people avoid argumentation due to a fear of criticism. Like argumentation, criticism has a negative undertone in our society. Both argumentation and criticism have tremendous benefits when they are done respectfully. Many of us are overly defensive when it comes to receiving criticism. We tend to have a knee-jerk reaction when we suspect someone is disrespecting us and intentionally hurting our pride. Often these suspicions turn out to be wrong, and those who have a strong unchecked initial reaction wind up looking foolish later. A rule in business is to wait 10-minutes before sending an angry e-mail. In most cases, the 10-minutes of cooling off encourage a rational and professional response over an angry one. It promotes a response that focuses on facts, rather than emotion. The following quotes provide wisdom in regard to criticism.

- "Don't mind criticism. If it is untrue, disregard it; if unfair, keep from irritation; if it is ignorant, smile; if it is justified it is not criticism, learn from it." — Unknown Source

- "Respond intelligently even to unintelligent treatment." — Lao Tzu (6th century B.C.)

- "To avoid criticism, do nothing, say nothing, be nothing." — Elbert Hubbard (1856-1915)

- "Whatever you do, you need courage. Whatever course you decide upon, there is always someone to tell you that you are wrong. There are always difficulties arising that tempt you to believe your critics are right. To map out a course of action and follow it to an end requires some of the same courage that a soldier needs. Peace has its victories, but it takes brave men and women to win them." — Ralph Waldo Emerson (1803-1882)

- "If I care to listen to every criticism, let alone act on them, then this shop may as well be closed for all other businesses. I have learned to do my best, and if the end result is good then I do not care for any criticism, but if the end result is not good, then even the praise of ten angels would not make the difference." — Abraham Lincoln (1809-1865)

In the late 1990s, I changed careers from manufacturing work to be an information technology consultant. In preparation, I obtained several technical certifications. There was a term for people that had the certifications but no real experience. They were "paper" certified. Don't be a "paper" anything, get the experience to supplement the paper or claim. If you are religious then be religious. Educate yourself in your religion. Read the religious doctrine and interpretation guides. Attend services and practice rituals. This may lead you in another direction, or it may lead you to a stronger connection with your faith then you ever had before.

I am an agnostic who promotes agnosticism. An agnostic promotes educated rational thinking over blind faith. An agnostic does not condemn any religion, but does hold morality and ethics over religious beliefs, and will condemn any religious practice that is blatantly immoral. An agnostic promotes truth. Truth is directly tied to morality according to Socrates. No matter who you are or what you practice, keep it real. Establish your foundation of belief on rock, not sand. This takes work. Do the work.

"The good life is one inspired by life and guided by knowledge."
– Bertrand Russell (1872-1970)

What is Truth?

"What is truth? Is truth unchanging law? We both have truths.
Are mine the same as yours?" (Andrew Lloyd Webber's Jesus
Christ Superstar, 1973)

As the primary goal of an agnostic is to discover truth, we should have a clear understanding of what truth is. For the vast majority of our history, it was a known fact the Earth was the center of the universe and that the universe circled the Earth. Despite the belief in this fallacy, past people and civilizations were actually much more in tune with the night skies then we are today. Of course they didn't have powerful telescopes, but the general population could see the stars and celestial objects much clearer in the night sky as they didn't have all the street lights interfering with the view. It was easily observed how the stars and moon would move across the sky at night as the sun moved across the sky by day. Why would anyone doubt the universe circled the Earth? For many thousands of years no one did.

The truths we have now are from observation, perception, experience, what we've been taught, and what we've been told. Our truths are different in certain respects as we are different, our perceptions are different. Everyone has a bias. For the agnostic the bias must be recognized and minimized. Sometimes our senses trick us, and what we've been taught and told turn out to be wrong. The world is filled with misinformation. This certainly does not mean the obtainment of true knowledge is impossible.

The purest truth can be found in mathematics because it is easily verifiable.

Truth in mathematics
1 plus 1 equals 2.
2 multiplied by 3 equal 6.
If A equals B, and B equals C, then C equals A.
If A is true, and B is unequal to A, then B is false.

Take the following example
A = Christianity
B = Hinduism
C = Confucianism
A is not equal to B. B is not equal to C. C is not equal to A.
If A is true then B and C are false.
If B is true then A and C are false.
If C is true then A and B are false.

Educated people of ancient civilizations were strongly connected to mathematics. They had to do math without computers. Think about how much mathematics were involved in designing and building the Great Pyramids roughly five thousand years ago. Finding truth often requires a creative mind to fit the right pieces together. The ancient Greeks loved geometry. Eratosthenes (276-195 B.C.) was the chief librarian in Alexandria, Egypt. By using geometric equation, two sticks, distance between the two, time of day and measurement of shadows, Eratosthenes accurately calculated the circumference of the Earth. During this time, many educated Greeks suspected the Earth was round, but didn't know how big it was. Eratosthenes found the true circumference by using mathematics and two sticks.

(About.com: Geography, Eratosthenes, http://geography.about.com/od/historyofgeography/a/eratosthenes.htm)

There are various methods for proving something is true. Mathematics may be the purest form but cannot be used for philosophical questions such as truths in morality. Other methods include:

- *The Socratic Method*
- *Scientific Method*
- *Expert opinion*
- *Common Sense*
- *Simplification*
- *Doing*

"The ideals which have always shone before me and filled me with the joy of living are goodness, beauty, and truth."
– Albert Einstein (1879-1955)

Socratic Method

Through examination Socrates guided people to find the answers themselves. Socrates would ask questions until his pupils discovered the truth they were seeking. Imagine being on the stand in a criminal trial getting cross examined by a prosecutor. This would be similar to answering questions under Socrates' scrutiny. The difference being the prosecutor's goal is to win his or her case while Socrates' goal is for you to find the truth.

Take an example of a speeding ticket where the police officer uses the Socratic Method:

- *Speeder* – I don't believe this ticket is fair because other people were speeding.
- *Officer* – Should I let everyone go as I can't pull everyone over at once?
- *Speeder* – I should be able to speed because I have a very long drive.
- *Officer* – So the law should only apply to people with short drives?
- *Speeder* – No, but the roads are dry and traffic is light, so I should be able to go above the speed limit.

- *Officer* – So the law should only be enforced when the roads are wet or by traffic conditions?

Anyone who's been through a court trial or has viewed real court trials on television or fictional ones on shows or movies has some familiarization with the Socratic Method. In the 1992 movie, *My Cousin Vinny,* the character Vinny Gambini is out to challenge the testimony of Mr. Tipton. Mr. Gambini recently acquired knowledge of southern grits and is going to leverage that education in his attack. Did Mr. Tipton really take five minutes to cook his breakfast? Is that the truth? What happens when this so called truth is challenged using the Socratic Method?

"*Vinny Gambini*: Is it possible the 2 defendants...

[*looks at judge*]

Vinny Gambini: went into the Sac-O-Suds, picked 22 specific items off of the shelf, had the clerk take the money, make change, then leave. Then 2 different men, drive up...

[*Seeing Mr. Tipton shake his head no*]

Vinny Gambini: Don't shake your head I'm not finished yet. Wait until you hear the whole thing you can understand what it is that I'm askin'. Then, two different men drive up in a similar looking car, go into the store, shoot the clerk, rob him, then leave?

Mr. Tipton: No. They didn't have enough time.

Vinny Gambini: Why not? How long was they in the store for?

Mr. Tipton: 5 minutes.

Vinny Gambini: 5 minutes? How do you know? Did you look at your watch?

Mr. Tipton: No.

Vinny Gambini: Oh, oh, oh, you tesitfied earlier that you saw the boys go into the store, and you had just begun to cook your breakfast and you were just getting ready to eat when you heard the shot.

Mr. Tipton: That's right.

Vinny Gambini: So obviously it takes you 5 minutes to cook your breakfast.

Mr. Tipton: That's right.

Vinny Gambini: That's right, so you knew that. You remember what you had?

Mr. Tipton: Eggs and grits.

Vinny Gambini: Eggs and grits. I like grits, too. How do you cook your grits? Do you like them regular, creamy or al dente?

Mr. Tipton: Just regular I guess.

Vinny Gambini: Regular. Instant grits?

Mr. Tipton: No self respectin' Southerner uses instant grits. I take pride in my grits.

Vinny Gambini: So, Mr. Tipton, how could it take you 5 minutes to cook your grits when it takes the entire grit eating world 20 minutes?

Mr. Tipton: I don't know, I'm a fast cook I guess.

Vinny Gambini: I'm sorry I was all the way over here I couldn't hear you did you say you were a fast cook, that's it?

Mr. Tipton: Yeah.

Vinny Gambini: Are we to believe that boiling water soaks into a grit faster in your kitchen than anywhere else on the face of the earth?

Mr. Tipton: I don't know.

Vinny Gambini: Well, I guess the laws of physics cease to exist on top of your stove. Were these magic grits? Did you buy them from the same guy who sold Jack his beanstalk beans?"
(The Internet Movie Database, Memorable quotes for My Cousin Vinny, http://www.imdb.com/title/tt0104952/quotes)

Scientific Method

This is a logical method that applies to natural law with the purpose of gaining knowledge through experimentation. This method does not apply to philosophical questions such as what is the proper definition of justice. Rene Descartes (1596-1650) attempted to apply scientific method to philosophy but was unsuccessful, for the most part, in making his theory popular. "Each problem that I solved became a rule which served afterwards to solve other problems." -- Rene Descartes. While Descartes' statement is good in theory and very much true in its own way, many philosophical arguments are too elusive for experiments and mathematical equations to solve.

The Scientific Method contains the following steps:

Step 1: Make an observation

Step 2: Ask a question
Step 3: Formulate a hypothesis
Step 4: Conduct an experiment – Variables must be controlled
Step 5: Analyze data and draw a conclusion

For example, let's come up with a theory that would have been considered ludicrous and even blasphemous a thousand years ago.

Step 1: Observation - The Earth spins on its axis and that is why from our point of view the Sun, Moon and stars move from one side of the sky to the other.

Step 2: Ask a Question – Why don't we feel the pull of the Earth's spinning? What effect does movement have on gravity? Do the rules of gravity apply to a moving object once it reaches speed as they do to an unmoving object?

Step 3: Formulate a Hypothesis – A baseball dropped from 10ft will behave identically on land as it would on a large ship moving 20mph.

Step 4: Conduct an Experiment – We drop a baseball from 10ft on land and record the results. The expected result is for the baseball to drop straight down. This is categorized as result A. We then drop the same baseball from 10ft on a ship moving 20mph and record the results. This is categorized as result B. Will the ball drop straight down or will the ball be directly affected by the speed of the ship?

Controlling the variables – The baseball must be dropped the same way on land and on ship. The wind conditions must be the same. The ship must be sailing on smooth waters. Choppy water and swaying could affect the results. The ship must be moving at a steady 20mph. Slowing down and speeding up the ship during the experiment may alter the results.

Step 5: Analyze Data and Draw a Conclusion – Both results of the land and ship experiments are the same. The baseball drops straight down. Once the ship gets up to speed the forces of gravity behave identically as if one was on land. This would explain how the Earth can spin over 700mph (speed depends on proximity to the equator) without everyone and everything flying off. If the Earth was to immediately stop, the surface would be completely rearranged, and we'd all be dead. It would be like getting into a car wreck going 700mph. (About.com: Geography, How fast does the earth spin? http://geography.about.com/library/faq/blqzearthspin.htm)

Expert Opinion

Often we take the opinion of an expert as fact. An expert is expected to have knowledge and experience making them a reliable source for information. If a great chef instructs you how to cook a particular meal you don't ask if they are sure or scrutinize them using the Socratic Method. You follow the instruction per the expert. In court trials experts are brought in to validate or dispute facts based on their expert opinion. Often we use criteria such as educational degrees and experience to determine if someone is, in fact, an expert. Unfortunately not all experts are created equally, and sometimes they disagree with each other. The vast majority of expert testimonial can be treated as fact; however, occasionally experts turn out to be wrong or express a distorted opinion based on an agenda rather than fact.

Occasionally, the credentials of experts are challenged. Once upon a time, the talk show commentator Oprah Winfrey had a child psychologist on her show dictating how parents should raise their kids. One of the parents asked the child expert how many kids she had. She didn't have any kids. After this statement, the child psychologist lost credibility with the audience members.

Common Sense

For practical reasons, we can't analyze everything for the best possible answer. Too much analysis creates the dreaded paralysis through analysis syndrome. If someone falls out of a tree they will likely be hurt. We don't need to ask experts or perform experiments as we simply know this through common sense. Common sense is an ability some people have over others. It can be a voice in your head sensing something isn't adding up. It can be directly tied to gut feelings and observation.

If you come home and someone you don't know is leaving your place with something that belongs to you, that someone is a thief. If home prices are growing 10% a year while income is growing 3% a year, the cycle is un-maintainable and a correction is inevitable. A US Congressman should read and understand a bill, before he or she votes on it. This is all common sense.

The comedian Chris Rock produced a skit on police brutality titled, "How to not get your ass kicked by the police." He referred to the work as a public service announcement. Although the intent is humor, the heart of the skit was common sense. When driving, if one simply pulls over at the request of a police officer rather than engaging in a high speed chase that endangers lives, they are infinitely less likely to get physically roughed up by the police.

Unfortunately, common sense is often ignored because it does not coincide with what we want or wish for. Often wishful thinking trumps common sense.

Simplification

How do you eat an elephant? One bite at a time. How do you solve a complex algebraic expression? You need to break it down. Often we need to break complex problems down into smaller digestible pieces in order to solve them. For example - very few of us are intimate with the financials of the federal government, but all of us are knowledgeable about the finances in our own household where many of the same rules apply. If you maintain a balanced budget, and your income increases while your debt remains the same, you can pay off debt and have more money on hand for buying stuff. If your income stays steady while your debts increase, and this becomes part of a long cycle, eventually you won't have enough money to pay the bills and each month you'll be sinking further and further in debt paying higher and higher interest charges. Like the federal government, your household can only maintain a certain amount of debt related to income.

In a mounting debt situation, you need to bring in more money, cut costs, or both. The federal government works by the same principles, and so do large corporations. Why do some corporations go bankrupt? They accumulated more debt than they could afford to pay through income, or their income dropped substantially where they could no longer pay their amount of debt. Any business losing money every quarter cannot continue the cycle and stay in business, just as any homeowner cannot continue to accumulate debt endlessly. By simplifying a problem or situation to something we can all understand; we are better able to deal with the situation and solve the problem.

Is ABC Corporation corrupt? How do we find out? Do we walk up to a large skyscraper with the ABC logo on it and ask the building if ABC Corporation is corrupt? Of course not as it is not a building that makes a corporation, it is people. We need to find out who's running ABC Corporation. Who are the chief executive officer, chief financial officer and other top executives? Who are the members of the board of directors? Who are the senior vice presidents? If the CEO and CFO are corrupt then ABC Corporation is corrupt until they replace the CEO and CFO. If the board of directors are corrupt then ABC Corporation is corrupt until somehow the board of directors are replaced, which is not an easy thing to do. If one senior vice president is corrupt then ABC Corporation is not corrupt, but does have a corrupt element that needs to be removed like a cancer. By tackling ABC Corporation as a company, we can't solve the problem. By breaking ABC down to the individual people that run it, we now have a practical approach for finding problems and solutions.

Doing

Sometimes one needs to do something in order to validate truth. How often does someone at the pool ask how cold the water is? What do they do next no matter what answer they are given? They put their foot in the water to find out for themselves.

The ancient Egyptians removed the brains of dead bodies before mummification. They believed thinking came from the heart, not the brain. How was this done? It appears mummification was a skill passed down from generation to generation. An exact step-by-step guide of human mummification does not exist although we do have clues from tomb paintings and research of the famous early historian Herodotus (484-430 B.C.). We also have documentation on how the sacred Apis bull was mummified. When it came to removing the brain, the popular theory was the brains were pulled out through the nose cavity with a hook.

In 1994, Professor Dr. Bob Brier performed the first mummification to an actual human cadaver in approx. 2,000 years. By actually performing the ancient Egyptian style mummification process hands on, Dr. Brier discovered the brains were not removed through the nose with a hook. The consistency of the brain made this technique impossible. The hook would not hold onto the brain matter. It appears the hook was used as a whisk to liquefy the brain, which was then poured out of the nose cavity by turning the cadaver over. There were many other discoveries and validations made during this modern mummification. This is an example of how sometimes actual doing is required to obtain the truth in the details.
(The Teaching Company, History of Ancient Egypt, Bob Brier)

"You know more of a road by having traveled it than by all the conjectures and descriptions in the world."
– William Hazlitt (1778-1830)

Truth can be complicated, but have faith in the obtainment of truth for much truth has been discovered through observation and philosophizing. Observing Earth's circular shadow on the moon during a lunar eclipse provided evidence that the world was round as did watching the sail of ships disappear as they headed for the horizon. We take knowledge that the world is round for granted as each one of us has seen pictures of the Earth from space. The technology to allow us this benefit is actually extremely recent in regard to human history.

We know the causes and the cures for many diseases. We know many facts regarding health and nutrition. We have gathered knowledge of ourselves as individuals and ourselves as groups of people. We continue to gather knowledge regarding DNA and evolution. We know much about our planet, the stars and the universe. We know much about plants and animals. Truth is obtainable, and with modern technology, we are discovering truths that people a hundred years ago could only dream of. Will we obtain undeniable facts regarding the existence of a higher being that even the most skeptical cannot deny? Time will tell.

PIECING TOGETHER LIFE AFTER DEATH

"I'm not afraid to die, I just don't want to be there when it happens."

– Woody Allen

Religion is the discipline of philosophy that provides answers to life after death and the purpose of mankind. It's time to take an agnostic approach towards religion. Let us empty our minds and begin with a solid foundation. A good initiation is a general study of major Eastern and Western faiths. This would be our broad and shallow Religion 101 foundation of knowledge. This education is everyone's individual journey. This is a solid beginning, and then obtaining deeper knowledge of a particular belief is the next logical step. One who is religious most likely has the answers to life after death they seek. For the religious, this exercise is not to obtain the answers to life after death, but to obtain further knowledge and fulfill curiosity.

Agnostic approach:

- *Begin with uncertainty and doubt, question everything*
- *Take a non-biased neutral approach*
- *Look at the situation from all angles*
- *Gather and validate the facts*

- *Make an informed decision*

First off, why does religion exist? Why does belief exist in all corners of the world in regard to an existence beyond the living? For many thousands of years supernatural belief has existed in all cultures. Is the reason survival instinct? Animals have survival instincts such as fight or flight response. These instincts only apply to staying alive. Animals do not foresee nor contemplate their own eventual death. Humans know everyone gets old and everyone will ultimately die. Can people cope with the possibility of their own eventual non-existence? Must they believe that their own existence goes on and on forever? Is there a logical foundation for this belief or is it all due to instinctive fear? What do we know about life after death? What do we know about the purpose for mankind?

There are hundreds of religions being practiced today, and thousands of beliefs that have come and gone over the centuries and millenniums. Some of the most popular religions at the time of this writing include Christianity, Islam, Hinduism, Buddhism, Confucianism and tribal religions. If we include ancient religions, five major theories of existence after death include:

- *Reincarnation* – When we die in one body, we are reborn in another body at birth.
- *Resurrection* – After death, we will eventually be brought back to life in the same body
- *Heaven and Hell* – After death, we either go to Heaven or Hell (some also believe in Purgatory as an in-between state)
- *The Spirit World* – After death we join the spirit world
- *Non-existence* – The end

Under the assumption these beliefs cannot all coexist as being true, than most or all are false. Perhaps we can rule out resurrection. The ancient Egyptians believed in resurrection and mummified pharaohs after they died and entombed them with treasure and their possessions. The mummified pharaohs would be well preserved, and have all their stuff upon eventual return to the living. Many of the wives and servants were also mummified close to the pharaoh. As stated earlier, upon mummification the brains were removed. During this time, it was a known fact that people thought with their hearts, not their brains. We still carry some of this belief in a non-literal sense today. The heart is associated with love. Non-existence was the alternative to resurrection. After death one either no longer existed, or would eventually be brought back to life as the Egyptian God Osiris was resurrected by his sister the Goddess Isis. If one wanted to make sure an enemy would not resurrect, they destroyed the body of their enemy.

The Egyptians were wrong. All the pharaohs who ruled Egypt for three thousand years are gone never to return, although many are preserved as mummies including Ramses II, also known as Ramses the Great. Ramses II is believed (backed up by evidence) to be the pharaoh in the story of Moses in the Old Testament. For those unfamiliar with the vastness of Egyptian history, Ramses II ruled during the 19th Dynasty (1279-1212 BC). Notice 19th Dynasty? The Great Pyramids were built approx. 1,500 years before Ramses the Great! The famous Greek pharaoh Cleopatra ruled over 1,000 years after Ramses II. She was the last pharaoh and died 30 years before Jesus Christ was born.

Let's move on to reincarnation. This belief is practiced in Eastern religions such as Hinduism and Buddhism. Before exploring reincarnation let's examine the belief in a soul or spirit. The soul or spirit is a belief that encompasses Eastern and Western religions including tribal beliefs. It means we have an existence beyond our physical bodies. Socrates himself had a spiritual belief and told his followers when he was dying it mattered not what was done with his body after death. Confucius believed our body and spirit must be whole when we present ourselves to our ancestors. This led to alternative medicine such as acupuncture, which was an alternative to surgery, which removes parts of the body. It also led to prosthetics so those with missing parts of the body could attempt, through artificial means, to be whole upon death and thereby present themselves whole to their spiritual ancestors.

In reincarnation, we are reborn after we die. Think of this as the flame of a candle being transferred to the wick of another candle. The burning flame is the soul while the candle is the physical body. The candle that burns twice as bright lasts half as long? In reincarnation, we are not simply reborn to whatever new life happens to be available during the time. The state of life we are reborn to depend on karma. Every cause has an effect. What goes around comes around. Good deeds produce good karma while bad deeds produce bad karma. The expression karma is an Eastern term; however, karma is a popular expression in Western society. It's a means of justice. Karma will determine the state of our rebirth after death and also has an impact on our current lives.

Is rebirth based on karma true justice? Can the state of our rebirths through karma be justice without memory of past sins or good deeds? Do we really gain knowledge with every rebirth as is foretold? Shouldn't this mean the human race would become wiser over time? Some critics maintain reincarnation was developed and promoted to suppress the poor. If you are born poor, it is because of wrong doings in a past life. It is your fault. Do not revolt against the wealthy, but rather live a good life and you'll be reborn under better circumstances.

For the most part, reincarnation is a never ending cycle. Very few have ended the cycle by reaching the ultimate state of mind and soul nirvana. The definition of the final state nirvana has to do with total enlightenment through the detachment of all desires. Nirvana exists in both Hinduism and Buddhism. For a Westerner in a capitalist economic system living in a prosperous nation, nirvana is a very difficult concept to grasp or connect with. Desire can bring pain as well as pleasure but does that make it evil? Is living life meditating and disconnecting from all desires the way to happiness and enlightenment, or should desire and passion be embraced as part of life?

It's time to move on from resurrection and reincarnation to heaven and hell. When I was a child this was explained as good people would go to heaven and bad people would go to hell. Later I found it was not quite that simple. In today's culture in America, overwhelmingly the term heaven refers to the Christian's heaven (also referred to as kingdom of God, paradise and the great reward). One can reach heaven through belief in Jesus Christ as the son of God, repenting of sins, and to spread the word of Jesus. The exact rules for reaching heaven may vary slightly from denomination or sect (ex. Is baptism required?) Heaven is a beautiful wondrous place where our soul can feel God's direct presence and glory. Heaven is where God and the angels reside. There is no sin in heaven. This is also no sickness or pain, no sorrow or crying or mourning, no more hunger, thirst and death. Heaven is an exclusive place for the righteous, the wicked will not enter.

Now for the place that's not so nice. Before hell let's explore Hades.

In Greek mythology Hades was the brother of Zeus and son of Kronos, who was overthrown by his sons allowing Zeus to take the throne. The universe was divided and Zeus took the sky while Hades took the underworld and Poseidon took the sea.

The dead went to Hades. Their souls were transported across the river Styx. Hades was a place for the dead but not a place of punishment. Hell is a place of punishment. The biblical descriptions of hell include fire and brimstone, fiery oven, judgment by fire and eternal punishment. Punishment includes weeping and gnashing of teeth and no rest day and night. This is where souls go who in life didn't take the appropriate steps for heaven. Other condemnations aside from non-believers include murderers, thieves, witches, sorcerers and prostitutes. Greed, sexual immorality, jealousy, drunkenness and lying can also land one into the fiery pits. (Evidence for God, What will Hell be Like? http://www.godandscience.org/doctrine/hell.html)

The Italian Catholic poet Dante Alighieri (1265-1321) wrote of nine circles of hell in his first canticle *Inferno* of his work *Divine Comedy*. He used biblical scripture and Greek mythology in his work. As the story goes, Dante is guided through hell by his dearly departed love Beatrice and ancient roman poet Virgil (70-19B.C.). Hell is shaped like a funnel and inside are circles spiraling down to the center.

Circle 1: Limbo – This is where sinless philosophers and pagans reside. Aristotle, Plato and Socrates are here because they were not baptized and didn't worship God's trinity.

Circle 2: The Lustful – For those who acted on lust over reason. Residents include Cleopatra and Achilles.

Circle 3: The Gluttonous – For those who spent their lives constantly eating and drinking to excess. Punishment includes freezing rain and getting chewed on by Cerberus the three headed dog.

Circle 4: Hoarders and Wasters – For misers who simply amassed wealth for themselves during their lifetime, and those who spent everything they had on frivolous material objects and things. Punishment includes eternally pushing around heavy boulders.

Circle 5: The Styx – For those who are wrathful. Punishment includes the souls of wrath viciously and relentlessly attacking each other in the murky waters of the Styx.

Circle 6: City of Dis – For the heretics which are those who deny God's existence. Punishment includes laying in burning hot iron tombs, which will be sealed forever upon judgment day.

Circle 7: The Violent – For those when living was violent towards their neighbors, violent towards their self (suicide), and violent towards God. Punishment varies upon sin and includes forever drowning in a boiling river of blood, existing as a tree which regenerating leaves and branches are eternally and painfully eaten by Harpies and laying on burning hot sand.

Circle 8: Malebolge – For the fraudulent. There are many punishments depending on the fraud committed. Punishment includes getting eternally hacked up into pieces and being sunk in a river of excrement.

Circle 9: Cocytus – For the treacherous. This circle is frigidly cold and home of Satan. Punishment includes entombment in ice unable to move or speak. Satan has three mouths that endlessly chew on three sinners; Brutus and Cassius who betrayed and killed Julius Caesar and Judas Iscariot, who betrayed Jesus.

(Dante's Inferno, A Virtual Tour of Hell, http://web.eku.edu/flash/inferno)

Obviously, by any account hell is an awful place. Do Christians believe all the non-Christians are all going to hell? There appears to be division within the faith regarding this. Most Christians do not believe the billions of people who were born and raised under a different religion are condemned to hell. Some dogmatic Christians, however, are not as forgiving. The Bible states that God will judge all people righteously. Jesus preaches tolerance and forgiveness. Allah is proclaimed as forgiving and merciful repeatedly in the Qur'an. When religions preach tolerance, mercy and forgiveness but then are oppressively intolerant of other religions and beliefs a major contradiction is revealed, in my opinion.

Now let's explore the spirit world. The spirit or soul is separate from the body. It contains the essence of who we are and is immortal. As stated earlier, the belief in the spirit appears to transcend the vast majority of the religions. Like the body, the soul can be hurt and can be healed. It's important to keep both body and soul healthy. The birth of the soul differs in religion. In Islam the soul was born with the body while in Hinduism the soul was born at the beginning of time.

Spiritualists believe the living can communicate with spirits. A medium or person of spiritual ability can communicate with the spirits through séances. Unfortunately, many séances held to communicate with the dead have been tied to fraud. The paranormal spirit world may be real. Scientists called parapsychologists study events that cannot be accounted for by natural law. They study perception beyond the five senses such as telepathy and clairvoyance.

Can the soul existing separately from the body be proven? One of the most prominent sources of knowledge at the time of this writing is the study of near-death experience. People have recorded out of body experiences while brain dead (literally) such as witnessing events or overhearing conversations away from their bodies that were later verified to be true. Dr. Raymond Moody studied 150 people who had clinically or nearly died and reported his findings. He concluded nine common experiences, which are:

1. Hearing strange sounds
2. Feelings of peace
3. Feelings of painlessness
4. Out-of-body experiences
5. Experiencing a tunnel vortex
6. Rising into the heavens
7. Seeing a bright light and beings of light
8. Experiencing a life review
9. Reluctance to return

(Scientific Evidence for Survival of Consciousness after Death, http://www.near-death.com/evidence.html)

These experiences were common regardless of race, cultural background or religious orientation. The evidence against the soul is brain injury. Brain imbalance, disease and injuries have been proven to impair intelligence, and change personalities. If the soul is separate from the physical brain how can this be? Perhaps when the physical brain is damaged the vehicle in which the soul interacts with the living is damaged and therefore, the soul is unable to represent itself properly?

Do the spirits have any attachment or influence towards the living world? Those who practice ancestor worship certainly believes so and certainly so do those who believe in ghosts. Ancestor worship or reverence exists in many tribal religions including African and Native American. It also exists in Chinese and Japanese culture. There were also ancient Greek and Roman followers. The souls of our ancestors can bring us good fortune and strength. They can also bring about bad luck. We need to perform the right rituals to gain the favor and thereby resulting good fortune and fate of our departed family members.

And now let's explore the unpopular belief of non-existence after death, the ultimate equalizer of man.

"This is the end, beautiful friend
This is the end, my only friend, the end."
                                (The Doors, The End, 1967)

"All those moments will be lost in time, like tears in rain. Time to die."
                                (The movie Blade Runner, 1982)

The ancient Egyptians believed in two fates, resurrection and death. As it appears no one resurrected, all the ancient Egyptians no longer exist in any state according to their own belief. What would it mean if there is no life after death? Would people do more with their lives knowing it was all they had?

What is the agnostic conclusion to life after death? There is no standard answer, only opinions and theories that differ from any organized religion. I will give my own theory. First I should admit my own biases. Life is a blessing where we can enjoy the greatest pleasures and passion. Life is a curse where we suffer the greatest pain, and in that every life ends. Death is a blessing when it ends constant suffering and allows living beings to rest in peace. Death is a curse when lives are cut short. We mourn the death of our pets. When loved ones die, part of our spirit dies with them. Humans do not life nearly long enough. We all age much too quickly. Aging is an incurable disease. Thoughts of my eventual death haunt me constantly. The clock is always ticking, and nothing lasts forever. Despite all my personal feelings about aging and death, it's not in me to believe in something out of fear or convenience, no matter how much my thoughts of mortality grieves me.

"Life's tragedy is that we get old too soon and wise too late."
-- Benjamin Franklin (1706-1790)

The planets and the stars don't last forever. Will the universe eventually cease to exist, or is it caught in an eternal cycle? The stars are not constant and will burn out eventually. If the theory of the big bang is true, is it the beginning of a cycle? Right now the universe is expanding rapidly. Will there come a time when the universe retracts? Will there be a time when the universe is compacted into a great black hole until the contraction is so great a new big bang is created? Could there be a constant cycle of big bangs with nothing surviving from one to the other, and all matter eventually broken down into the most basic element hydrogen?

"This thing all things devours; Birds, beasts, trees, flowers; Gnaws iron, bites steel; Grinds hard stones to meal; Slays king, ruins town, And beats mountain down."
(J.R.R. Tolkien, The Hobbit, 1937)

Does anything survive over vast amounts of time? Gods such as the mighty Zeus have been transformed from immortal Gods people worshiped into mere story book characters over time. Is there any logical basis for life after death? Does an eternity in heaven or hell due to an existence of roughly 30-90 years on Earth have any logical bearing? Would the great creator or creators of life really want to deal with all the administration over who goes where after death? Do not humans live and die during their own lifetime? The child becomes an adult.

We are all individuals, but we are also influenced by our environment and experiences. Some people have many mental challenges to deal with that came at birth or at a later time by injury or disease. When people change, what version of their self goes on after death if any? "Lather was thirty years old today, they took away all of his toys." (Jefferson Airplane, Lather, 1968) Perhaps Lather will get his toys back at the mental institution he was committed to, or in the afterlife. Some people appear to remain the same from childhood to the grave. Their demeanor, mannerisms and personality stays constant. Others appear to change dramatically in every aspect. Sometimes major life events or simply getting older changes the way we think and who we are. Sometimes the person known in high school is unrecognizable 15 years later.

When facts are absent theories are required. The following is my own personal view. I am interested in further research and possible conclusions regarding near death experiences. I'm keeping an open mind to new discoveries. At this time, I'm not convinced there is anything beyond this world. The only way to immortality that I know of right now is for science to pinpoint the exact cause that makes us age, and to find a way to stop and perhaps even reverse the process. There are many guides on living long and healthy, but no considerable breakthroughs at the time of this writing for a substantial increase in life expectancy. The maximum life expectancy in humans is estimated to be approx. 120 years. The life expectancy in America in the year 2000 is 78 or approx. two-thirds the maximum. This is a substantial increase from a 47 year life expectancy in the year 1900. So it appears, we've become at least a little less mortal then we once were.

So what difference does anything make if there is no afterworld? Would this mean we should care more or less about ourselves and others? Does this mean we should care more or less about morality and justice? We're not dead yet. Perhaps everything we see, do, think, and all our memories will eventually be lost in time, like tears in the rain, as if they never existed in the first place, but we are not dead yet. We can still make a difference in this world. Whether you believe in the afterlife or not, there is no reason not to live a full just life, a good life.

I maintain that good people will do good and evil people will do evil. They will find a reason to act upon who they are. Then there are the indifferent people who will act like sheep not noticing, caring or acting upon what's happening in their community, country and the world. Who are you? I will act upon the side of good because that is who I am. I am far from perfect and certainly no saint, but I do strongly believe in freedom and a high standard of living for all people. My own mission will not change regardless of the existence or non-existence of an afterlife. For now the agnostic approach falls short of definitively answering the question of life after death. I will most likely die not knowing the true answer, but there is always hope.

"Immortality is a long shot, I admit. But somebody has to be first."
— Bill Cosby

How to Die

"In my own life if I knew I was going to pass away I'd love to sit down and resolve every issue so I could go peacefully."
— John Travolta

My grandmother-in-law passed away a few years ago. She died peacefully knowing she would be with the Lord in heaven. My grandfather-in-law lives in a small place and doesn't have many possessions. Everything related to what he has are all in an envelope in his dresser. He has made out his will. As he puts it, any idiot would be able to figure out any and all of his remaining business when he dies. He will eventually die in peace knowing he will be with the Lord in heaven and reunited with his wife of over 60 years.

(My wife's grandparents when they were young and newly married- Pictures are from the early 1940s)

My own grandmother on my mother's side didn't die as peacefully.

My mother told me of her final state of mind before she passed. She was angry and bitter towards her deceased ex-husband of whom she divorced and hadn't seen for over 20 years. My mother told me she didn't want to die like her mother, and I know she won't. She is not an angry and bitter person and in fact, is the complete opposite.

My father died when he was seven years older than I am now at the young age of 46. He was a depressed alcoholic on disability. At 41 he was diagnosed with progressive heart disease and given approx. 5 years to live at the time, which turned out to be accurate. Just before getting diagnosed, for whatever reason, he had canceled his life insurance policy. My memories of my father are not good. His own father left him before he was born. He never got over this and carried it as a burden his entire life. So much for time healing all wounds, it doesn't.

Although initially successful and accomplished without even a high school diploma, he lacked confidence and was intimidated by people who had a college degree. He died peacefully in his sleep. Because of a falling out, I had not spoken to him in about 6 months before his death. For those who have cried and were deeply saddened at their own fathers passing, feel glad as this meant your relationship was something special. Many people would give much to have your tears.

A few years ago, a man who worked for the same company and in the same office as I did committed suicide. I didn't know him, but a close friend of his gave me the details. Apparently, he turned down an advancement opportunity and then changed his mind when it was too late. I'm not sure if this was the exact reason he took his own life, but apparently he was deeply depressed about the whole situation. He was married and had a baby daughter. He took his own life by shooting himself in the head in his basement. His wife found his body the next morning. People who described the funeral stated his widow was still in shock. She looked tortured, sad and confused.

It was difficult for me to hear people speak kindly of this man. It was hard for me to listen to, but I bit my tongue. I didn't know this man but knew his actions and had nothing but disgust for what he did. How could he do this to his wife and daughter? All I could think about was his poor wife and daughter, and how they were going to carry on. For the most part, suicide is a detestable selfish act, especially by those who take others with them.

Many die peacefully, some die angry and bitter, some take their own lives and some die by doing very stupid things. The people who die doing stupid things have a chance at fame by making what's known as the Darwin Awards. Yes, there is an organization that records the dumbest deaths and the details around these incidents can be found at www.darwinawards.com. Deaths include breaking into a lion's den at the zoo and messing with the lion. These fatalities often involve large consumptions of alcohol.

All we know is the lives we have lived. Death can be scary and even terrifying. Socrates used to mock people who feared death as they were ignorant as to whether or not death was better or worse than living.

"To fear death, my friends, is only to think ourselves wise, without being wise: for it is to think that we know what we do not know. For anything that men can tell, death may be the greatest good that can happen to them: but they fear it as if they knew quite well that it was the greatest of evils. And what is this but that shameful ignorance of thinking that we know what we do not know?" – Socrates (469-399 B.C.)

Further argument that death should not be feared is in the Socratic Paradox. Evil is ignorance and good is knowledge. God is good and therefore, the world is good. God is good and does not harm. A soul cannot be helped or improved in a place such as hell, and it does a soul harm to be in hell. It neither benefits the soul of man nor the soul of God. In a good world, no harm can come to a good person.

So did Socrates stick to his guns after he was sentenced to death, or did he recant and begin praying to the Greek Gods? His previous quote was actually taken during his trail. Many people believe that when faced with danger and death, the non-religious become religious, and the religious become more devout. In the face of death, all the sudden the atheists start praying to God. For the most part, this may be true; however, some are brave and carry their convictions to the end regardless of circumstances. Socrates was just as brave facing death as he was in his quest for truth. His final words can be found in his most accomplished student Plato's work titled *The Apology*.

It's important to note apology in Greek translates to defense. By no means did Socrates admit to any wrong doings. He was charged by the Athenian court with the crimes of not recognizing the Gods of the

State, inventing new deities and corrupting the youth. In his defense, the piety of Socrates can be found in the following quote:

"Good sir, you are an Athenian, a citizen of the greatest city with the greatest reputation for both wisdom and power; are you not ashamed of your eagerness to possess as much wealth, reputation, and honors as possible, while you do not care for nor give thought to wisdom or truth, or the best possible state of your soul?"

Socrates defends himself well and honorably. He does not apologize in our sense of the word and even attempts to humiliate his accusers. Ultimately, the deck is stacked against him. He has made fools of powerful men, and these men take their vengeance upon him. Socrates is sentenced to death and drinks the poison hemlock. He accepts the verdict and makes no plea for mercy. What are the last words of Socrates? "Crito, I owe a rooster to Asclepius; will you remember to pay the debt?"

My grandfather-in-law is 87 years old. He still drives a car and lives alone unassisted. He does not take any prescription drugs and is very rarely sick. He attributes this to being a farmer when he was younger. What I've learned from him is that farmers are the hardest workers in the world and no winters were as cold when he was younger and no summers as hot. We young people don't know what work and cold and heat really are. The great comedian Bill Cosby in his work titled, *Himself,* discusses what his father used to tell him. Apparently, Mr. Cosby's father had to walk miles to school barefoot in the snow, uphill both ways. Now the non-farmers and meteorologists may disagree with some of my grandfathers' claims, but most of the time we simply allow him to get his own way.

There are many that spend their final years as complete dependants. They rely on others to do everything for them as they are unable to physically care for themselves. There are many reasons for this. Some reasons are disease or injury. Other reasons include not maintaining a healthy lifestyle earlier that would have led to an independent life later. For the later it's a tragedy; final years of limited enjoyment of life, a burden to other people, and a strain to the country's healthcare system that could have been prevented. It's important we make the right choices now to be healthy later.

How do we want to be remembered after we die? Do we want a large gathering at our funeral or just a few close relatives and friends? What do we want said of us when we die? Ideally, one will be remembered and one will be loved after death.

- "Die when I may, I want it said of me by those who knew me best, that I always plucked a thistle and planted a flower where I thought a flower should grow." – Abraham Lincoln (1809-1865)
- "Let us endeavor so to live that when we come to die even the undertaker will be sorry." – Mark Twain (1835-1910)

I have listed personal stories and various outside sources related to the subject of how to die. Some of my own personal stories are unique while others are common. So what is the great conclusion? Everyone should contemplate how to die at one time or another. This is a personal decision that each of us should eventually prepare for. Not everything can be resolved using an agnostic approach or any other kind of rationality. Some things need to be resolved from the heart. The following is how I intend to die:

- Without fear, brave like Socrates
- Without regret, anger and bitterness
- At peace as my wife's grandmother died through means of strength in my own beliefs as she had in hers
- Not dying by doing something really stupid
- Making sure all my remaining business is easily attended to by my survivors through means such as having a living will and trust.
- I want to be remembered as Abraham Lincoln wanted to be remembered as being someone who planted a flower where I thought a flower should grow.
- I want to be completely independent through to my final days by maintaining a lifestyle that promotes health in the body and in the mind. If a horrible disease such a cancer or an accident prevents the obtainment of my wish, then succumbing to an undesirable fate beyond my means is more acceptable than succumbing to an undesirable fate within my means.
- I want to be remembered and loved after I die by those who

knew me well.

- I want those who knew me well to be sad at my passing but happy in my memories

Will my plan on how to die eventually be followed and fulfilled? My hope is not to find out for a very long time.

THE ETERNAL STRUGGLE OF GOOD AND EVIL

- "In spite of everything I still believe that people are really good at heart. I simply can't build up my hopes on a foundation consisting of confusion, misery and death." – Anne Frank (1929-1945)
- "Wicked men obey from fear; good men, from love." – Aristotle (384-322 B.C.)

There have been many long discussions over many generations in regard to good and evil. These discussions must continue, and continue often. How do we know who we are without scrutinizing what is good, and what is evil? What is the agnostic standpoint? The agnostic approach is difficult as this discussion is subjective. In the spirit of an agnostic approach, I will provide various sources in my analysis. I have a strong bias of good over evil as innately I am a good person. I'm a student of the great ancient Eastern and Western philosophers who were among the most moral and ethical people who ever lived. I follow the wisdom of Socrates that knowledge is good and ignorance is bad. Good is directly related to truth. Knowledge promotes morality while ignorance promotes corruption. The purpose of an agnostic is to obtain and promote truth, which is to obtain and promote what is good. What is good often differs from what is popular. So where do good and evil come from?

Good and evil exists in the animal and human world. There are insects and animals that have both good and evil traits and instincts. As the most advanced species on Earth, humans are able to magnify the good and evil that exists in animals. So what is good and what is evil? Are the definitions constant or do they change based on ruling party, society or religious views and customs? I and many philosophers past and present maintain that there are concrete definitions of good and evil. I don't subscribe to the "might makes right" school of thought. I believe in right makes might. There are actions that are wrong regardless of anything. Acceptance of evil does not make evil good. The definition and impact of evil does not change due to ignorance.

> "Freedom is not the right to do what we want, but what we ought. Let us have faith that right makes might and in that faith let us; to the end, dare to do our duty as we understand it." – Abraham Lincoln (1809-1865)

Good is to create and do good by oneself, ones' family and society. Evil is to destroy and do evil by oneself, ones' family and society. There is some evil in good and some good in evil. A new tree in a crowded forest can only live and grow if another tree dies to let in needed sunlight. Sometimes creation requires destruction. Plant eaters need predators to keep their population steady or the plant eaters over populate and destroy all the vegetation. There is a balance of creation and destruction in nature. Often a society becomes closer and stronger when faced with an evil threat or action. Often a good society can become complacent and lazy when unthreatened allowing evil to grow from within un-noticed and unchallenged until it is deeply rooted.

Taoism (also known as Daoism) is an early Chinese religion which emphasizes a balance between humans and nature. One must be flexible and go with the flow. Taoism is represented by the Ying Yang symbol.

The black (Ying) and white (Yang) represent polar opposites, such as but not specifically good and evil. The symbol also represents the balance between each. There will always be good and always be evil. One cannot exist without the other. Chi is believed to be a vital energy in all things. It's important to allow this energy to properly flow in the body and in the world. Tai Chi is an ancient Chinese exercise that promotes the balance of Chi in the body. Feng Shui is the art of allowing Chi to flow properly in ones' environment.

Taoism is the practice of peacefully living in a world of opposing forces such as good and evil. It's a faith that when good and evil are out of balance, the balance will return. Go with the flow. In Taoism, it's important to be flexible. A belief shared by famous martial artist Bruce Lee as he explains how to overcome obstacles.

"Be like water making its way through cracks. Do not be assertive, but adjust to the object, and you shall find a way round or through it. If nothing within you stays rigid, outward things will disclose themselves.

Empty your mind, be formless. Shapeless, like water. If you put water into a cup, it becomes the cup. You put water into a bottle and it becomes the bottle. You put it in a teapot it becomes the teapot. Now, water can flow or it can crash. Be water my friend."

(Bruce Lee, 1940-1973)

Taoism addresses good and evil and provides a method for living with them. There is a balance that exists between all extremes. I use the example of the pendulum to represent balance in the world. When the pendulum is center there is balance. The object is perfectly aligned with its' true value. When the pendulum is to the right the object is overvalued. There will be a correction in which the value lessens. When the pendulum is to the left the object is undervalued. There will be a correction in which the value increases. Think of the stock market and real estate market. The pendulum is always swinging back and forth. When the market is calm and rational, the pendulum swings slowly in short distances. When the market is in chaos the pendulum swings wildly in large distances.

When the pendulum is out of balance the best solution is a controlled adjustment. This takes a proactive future looking approach. Unfortunately, many leaders are short sighted and only concerned with near future. They then have to react to unforeseen required adjustments without planning, and disastrous results as consequence. An example would be a president claiming seven hundred billion dollars is needed right now to save the economy.

"Order marches with weighty and measured strides. Disorder is always in a hurry." – Napoleon Bonaparte (1769-1821)

War and peace do not last forever. When there is war have faith that there will be peace. When there is peace one must be vigilant of conflict and war. There are some things that are out of our control. We must do what we can to fight the good fight. We must also have faith that when things are bad, they will get better.

Personally, I have been stabbed in the back by family members and business associates many times. There are many people throughout my life who have done me wrong. There are exponentially far more people throughout my life that have done me right. You will not always have an opportunity to confront people who were intentionally harmful due to many circumstances including timing, location and politics. You will not always have an opportunity to thank people who have been kind and generous. When situations like this occur, we need to have faith that there will be a balance. What goes around comes around. One way or another, justice will be served. For the people who have done us wrong, either we let it be, or hold onto the anger and injustice. Often we do hold on to anger, but it subsides over time. I'm not a believer that time heals all wounds; however, it can take the edge off of the pain.

"*Ronny Cammareri*: I ain't no freakin' monument to justice! I lost my hand! I lost my bride! Johnny has his hand! Johnny has his bride! You want me to take my heartache, put it away and forget?" (The movie Moonstruck, 1987)

"When I find myself in times of trouble
Mother Mary comes to me
Speaking words of wisdom, let it be"
(The Beatles, Let It Be, 1970)

Do good and evil exist in the animal world? I would argue they absolutely do. The varieties in animal life on Earth are miraculous. Animals exist that can produce light, see with sonar, spin webs and can change color to camouflage with their surroundings. We have predators and we have prey. There are plant eaters that do not harm other animals, and there are meat eaters that take lives. We have alligators, sharks, piranhas and mosquitoes. We have swans, dolphins, deer and fireflies. There are animals that represent all the good and bad qualities of man, from unconditional protective love to thoughtless destruction.

An example of an evil behavior in animals is the Brown-headed Cowbird. This bird does not build a nest of its own but lays eggs in the nests of other bird species. The eggs typically hatch earlier than the host eggs and the cowbird chicks' rapid growth allows the monopoly of food and space in the nest. The host's chicks usually die by starvation or by being pushed out of the nest. The mother of the hijacked nest winds up raising the cowbirds that murdered her chicks.

An example of good in animals is the dolphin. Dolphins never attack humans and have been known since ancient Greek times to rescue people from drowning and even protecting people from sharks. In 2008 dolphins rescued two beached whales in New Zealand by guiding them to open waters. Dolphins have also safely guided ships through uncharted waters.

Humans don't seem to consider whether an animal is good or evil. We destroy with reckless abandon based on greed. This was all too evident when American buffalo was slaughtered for their skin while their bodies were left rotting in the plains. Japanese dolphin hunts slaughter thousands of dolphins every year. In Africa, families of apes are being hunted. Should certain species be protected over others? I believe so.

When someone butchers a chicken the thought that comes to my head is that this was done by a farmer. When someone butchers an ape the thought that comes to my head is that this was done by a murderer. Is this my own emotional bias? Of course, but none of our emotional feelings should simply be dismissed, even though they may come from the heart rather than the brain. We are not machines, we are humans. Recognizing our biases to promote a fair and balanced view does not necessarily mean dismissing our biases completely.

Let's look at characteristics that are good and that are evil. The evil characteristics include some of those mentioned in the Bible that could land you into the fiery pits of hell. As evil is too strong of a term for many of the negatively categorized characteristics, I will use the term "bad" characteristics. The following list and analysis are subjective and my own opinion. Everyone should individually go through this exercise at some time to obtain a clear personal definition of good and evil character. Good and bad characteristics include:

Good Characteristic	Synonyms	Bad Characteristic	Synonyms
Strong	tough	Weak	fragile
Generous	Big hearted, giving, charitable	Selfish	Self-centered
Aware	Conscious, Alert	Ignorant	Unaware, uninformed
Humble	modest	Arrogant	Conceited, big headed
Courage	brave	Cowardice	spinelessness
Tolerant	Understanding, charitable, forgiving	Intolerant	Prejudiced, narrow-minded, unsympathetic
Kindness	Compassion, empathy, sympathy, considerate	Wickedness	Sinful, immoral, cruel
Contentment	Satisfaction, happiness	Greed	Gluttony, self-indulgence
Respect	Admiration, reverence	Jealousy	Envious, resentful
Integrity	Honesty, truthfulness, reliability	Dishonesty	Deceit, fraudulence, corruption

Strong and Weak

In order to claim that one is better than the other, this analysis is based on mankind being generally good and strength and weakness is in regard to good people. The terms strong and weak are not in regard to physical strength. Strong and weak are to describe determination, willpower and resolve. Why is this important? Strong willpower is required to fight evil. "All that is necessary for the triumph of evil is that good men do nothing." (Edmund Burke, 1729-1797) Strong determination triumphs physical strength. The Navy Seals are one of the elite fighting forces in the US. The trials to become a Seal are extremely tough. When analyzing those who have failed the test in comparison to those that have passed, there was a characteristic that was more attributed to success than physical strength that made the difference. It was mental toughness. It was determination.

In J. R. R. Tokens' *Lord of the Rings*, Gandalf was not strong enough to carry the corruptible ring of power. Instead of a mighty wizard the task went to a meek hobbit. The hobbit was not stronger in strength but stronger in resistance to corruption.

An example of weakness and how that relates to evil can be found in the Milgram experiment which began in 1961. It is unfortunate the footage of this experiment is not available to the general public at the time of this writing. Psychologist Stanley Milgram performed social psychological experiments to measure obedience to an authority figure. Unsuspecting subjects were hired to do a job they thought was to assist in the study of memory. The job was to punish someone for not correctly answering questions. In the experiment, there were three roles, the experimenter, the teacher and the learner. The job was to be a teacher (this is the subject of the experiment; the other two roles are cohorts and in on the experiment). The experimenter tells the teacher what to do and wears a lab coat.

The teacher has a panel of electric shock switches that are to be used when the learner gives the wrong answer or doesn't answer at all. In the original experiments, the learner who would receive the shocks was not visible. The learner was in a separate room with an audio connection. In later experiments the learner was visible and sometimes the teacher was required to force the learners arm down in order to receive a shock upon a wrong answer.

The results of this experiment were extremely disturbing. On the good side, there was a test subject who when told to apply the electric shock after hearing distress from the learner crossed his arms and refused. I don't recall the exact quote, but it was something like, "You can keep your money, I'm not going to do this." This is an example of someone who is strong. And then there was the test subject who kept applying the shocks up the scale even when the learner started to complain of chest pains and then eventually didn't respond at all. The man giving the shocks was reluctant, but when the experimenter offered to take full responsibility, the man acting as the teacher continued administering the punishment. At the end of the initial experiment, 26 out of 40 experiment participants applied the maximum voltage of 450-volts. The voltage shocks were not real, but the participants had no way of knowing this.

(About.com: Psychology, The Milgram Obedience Experiment, http://psychology.about.com/od/historyofpsychology/a/milgram.htm)

So how would you have done in this experiment? Would you go all the way up the scale, or would you have refused early on to apply an electric shock to another human being? Are you weak or are you strong? Everyday people are pressured into doing things they know are wrong, and that they will regret for the rest of their lives. Evil does not require a large membership. A few evil doers and a bunch of weak sheep is all that's required to perform unspeakable acts of evil. Be strong.

Generous and Selfish

The best example of generous and selfish is the character Ebenezer Scrooge in Charles Dickens' *A Christmas Carol*. Before visited by three spirits, Mr. Scrooge is as selfish as they come. He has plenty of money but hordes it. He won't even buy extra comforts for himself, let alone give to others around him of whom are in need. Why is this? Does he not recognize his own mortality? Does he not realize the only path this leads is dying with a whole lot of money that would then go somewhere else anyway? There is something that joins in Ebenezer's selfishness and that is misery. He seems to hate everyone including himself. He is alone and unhappy. Not only is he selfish with his money, he is selfish with his hospitality and friendship and love.

So is being selfish an evil trait? I would not say selfishness necessarily promotes evil, it just doesn't promote good. If we think about part of being good involving the promotion of happiness in ourselves and others; selfishness certainly doesn't do that. Selfishness should not be mistaken for cheap. Many people are generous with hospitality, friendship and love, but when it comes to money, they are tight fisted. This could be due to economic conditions. Many who lived through the depression are tight with money as the memory of barely scraping by when they had nothing is still strong. Many are generous with food, which is often an expression of love.

So what happens after the spirits visit Scrooge, and he realizes that he's not dead and has a chance of redemption? He experiences the greatest joy he's ever imagined. He becomes generous with his hospitality, friendship, love and his money. He spends a great deal of money on charity and the happiness of the people around him. He changes the fate of a lame boy who would have died without his help. He becomes an inspirational figure to his community. Ebenezer Scrooge is transformed from one who is miserable and alone to one who is happy and surrounded by people who love him.

This is a fictional character but many people are like the Scrooge before the transformation and the Scrooge after. Think about the selfish people you know. Are they happy? Think about the generous people you know. Are they happy? Overwhelmingly generous people are happier, and you don't need money to be generous. Often the most valuable thing we have is our time. Think about the elderly people who love you or did love you when they were living. They didn't want your money; they wanted your time, which brought them great happiness. Be generous.

Aware and Ignorant

We cannot fight evil if we are ignorant of where and when it is happening. The example I will give on awareness and ignorance, in regard to good and evil, is in the community. Aware means being aware of our surroundings and spending some time to keep up to date with what's happening in our community and the world. Before television, there were many more front porches. People would hang out on their front porches and say hello to everyone that walked by. They would also keep an eye out on the neighborhood.

Many people today don't leave their homes much. They are in front of television and computers most of the time. They are not aware of bad elements that may be entering their neighborhood. They don't know who their neighbors are. They live in isolation. As a result they are less in a position to look out for their neighbors and themselves. They are ignorant of their surroundings.

Spend some time saying hello to your neighbors. Attend neighborhood activities such as parties or association meetings. Get involved with community activities. Check out volunteer programs. Understand what threats and challenges are facing your neighborhood. Get information on illegal activity from your local police department. Getting a dog can help you meet neighbors and keep an eye on the neighborhood during dog walks. Often people who are aggressive about knowing what's going on are labeled busy bodies. A few busy bodies in a neighborhood are actually a very good thing. Be aware.

Humble and Arrogant

"I have been given the authority over you, and I am not the best of you. If I do well, help me; and if I do wrong, set me right. Sincere regard for truth."   – Abu Bakr (573-634)

Extreme arrogance is an evil trait and has done great wrong in this world since the beginning of civilization. Not only is it used to self-promote but also to tear down other groups of people. Somewhere and somehow it became hip to put down those in so called unskilled labor. Somehow it became hip to put down people who work in fast food restaurants. By far, the people who make arrogant statement about the millions and millions of people across the world in the food industry wouldn't last 5 minutes behind the grill or behind the register during the lunch time rush.

Every job requires training and every worker who puts in an honest day's work deserves respect. Many people in the low skilled market such as assembly line workers are using the opportunity as a stepping stone to higher paying jobs. They may be in a circumstance where money is needed to support themselves or their family while they try to take some night classes in order to move up in the job market. We do have people who enjoy working on the assembly line and other jobs that may not pay that well which is great as we need people to do that work. Not everyone wants to join the rat race, and that's fine as there is more room near the bottom of the ladder than there is at the top. The people who move up the ladder trade off more money for more responsibility and stress. Moving up the ladder may lead to nicer cars and bigger televisions, but by no means does it directly correspond to a happier life.

Arrogance is directly tied to ignorance and intolerance of people and ideas. When somebody thinks they know everything, they will not seek or accept knowledge or wisdom. Politicians who are arrogant will marginalize rather than respectfully address opposing points of views. Arrogant business leaders are not interested in hearing anyone else's opinion.

In the television series' Kitchen Nightmares, Chef Gordon Ramsay saves restaurants that are about to go under. The restaurant owners are often the chefs in the smaller establishments. You would think an owner would be humble having a successful mentor such as Mr. Ramsay help them save their restaurant, and thereby saving their family and everyone who works for them from financial ruin. Surprisingly, in many cases the owners are arrogant. With only a short period of time to turn the restaurant around, what technique does Gordon use to make the owner successful?

Chef Gordon Ramsay does not have a reputation for being a nice guy. The first thing he does when beginning the process of turning a restaurant around is to brutally humiliate the owner. He basically tells the owner he stinks, his food stinks and his restaurant stinks. Does Mr. Ramsay do this because he wishes to harm? The answer is no. One of the reasons for this approach is to entice passion from the owner. Get them to fight hard and work hard. The other necessity of this approach is that the arrogance of the owner needs to be purged. The owners will not learn if they believe themselves to be better than Chef Gordon Ramsay. The owners will not learn if they think of themselves as already possessing all the knowledge and wisdom necessary to run a successful business.

The humiliation the owner receives from Mr. Ramsay is proportionate to their own arrogance. The more arrogance, the more humiliation is administered. It is only after the arrogance is removed or at least diminished, that Gordon is able to build them back up and mentor these owners in what they need to do in order to be successful, and save their establishments. The method he uses for training restaurant owners and chefs is similar to the way soldiers are trained in boot camp. Drill Sergeants do not have a reputation for being nice either.

"Many people might have attained wisdom had they not assumed they already had it."   – Unknown Source

Arrogance should not be confused with confidence. To be confident simply means you are prepared for a challenge and expect yourself to do well. You might expect to beat people in a competition not because you are superior to them, but simply better skilled and better prepared for the specific challenge. We are all human with our own strengths and weaknesses. It's important to remember that just because someone is great at something does not mean they are great at everything. I remember a news segment on Bill Wellington's hamburger recipe. Bill was a center for the Chicago Bulls during the later 1990s championship years with basketball great Michael Jordan. A news reporter asked Bill if he was asserting that his hamburgers were better than Michael Jordan's. Bill responded stating Michael was a better basketball player than he was but that didn't mean Michael was better at everything.

A lesson in humility is taught in the following story "The Monk and the Samurai" retold by John Porcino:

There was once a samurai warrior who traveled to the distant home of an old monk. On arriving he burst through the door and bellowed, "Monk, tell me! What is the difference between heaven and hell?"

The monk sat still for a moment on the tatami-matted floor. Then he turned and looked up at the warrior. "You call yourself a samurai warrior," he smirked. "Why, look at you. You're nothing but a mere sliver of a man!"

"Whaaat!!" cried the samurai, as he reached for his sword.

"Oho!" said the monk. "I see you reach for your sword. I doubt you could cut off the head of a fly with that."

The samurai was so infuriated that he could not hold himself back. He pulled his sword from its sheath and lifted it above his head to strike off the head of the old monk. At this the monk looked up into his seething eyes and said, "That, my son, is the gate to hell." Realizing that the monk had risked his life to teach this lesson, the samurai slowly lowered his sword and put it back into the sheath. He bowed low to the monk in thanks for this teaching.

"My friend," said the monk, "That is the gate to heaven."
(www.healingstory.org/peace_tales/hsa_peace_stories.html)

Socrates was humble in confession of his own ignorance. When business leaders are humble they are open to better ideas and solutions. When politicians are humble the country is less polarized and divided. Be humble.

Courage and Cowardice

"A fight is not won by one punch or kick. Either learn to endure or hire a bodyguard. Forget about winning and losing; forget about pride and pain. Let your opponent graze your skin and you smash into his flesh; let him smash into your flesh and you fracture his bones; let him fracture your bones and you take his life. Do not be concerned with escaping safely - lay your life before him." – Bruce Lee (1940-1973)

Most people are not as courageous as the legendary Bruce Lee; however, often having courage is about having someone's back rather than being in the front lines of confrontation. When someone does wrong, often it becomes the responsibility of another to make it right. This takes courage, but may also take diplomacy. Many people are intimidated by confrontation, but they will rise to the challenge if necessary.

Courage can involve standing up to bullies or rising up to extraordinary challenges. Courage is often associated with our military personnel and police officers. Socrates showed courage by challenging the wisdom of powerful men. The passengers of United Flight 93 on 9/11/2001 showed courage. They tried to overtake the terrorists who had hijacked their plane. The plane crashed without carrying out the terrorist's mission. Let's not forget the courageous heroes of Flight 93 and the many others like them.

What would you do if someone unjustly insulted your friend in public? What would you do if someone physically assaulted your friend or a stranger in public? What would you do if you were assaulted? Often we suffer when someone's cowardice allows evil to survive and continue unchecked. People who don't report or act on wrong doings have responsibility when that same wrong doing is allowed to continue and victimize others. Have courage.

"To know what is right and not do it is the worst cowardice."
– Confucius (551-479B.C.)

Tolerant and Intolerant

- "I would like to be known as a person who is concerned about freedom and equality and justice and prosperity for all people." – Rosa Parks (1913-2005)
- "The highest result of education is tolerance." – Helen Keller (1880-1968)
- "The legitimate powers of government extend to such acts only as are injurious to others. But it does me no injury for my neighbour to say there are twenty gods, or no god. It neither picks my pocket nor breaks my leg."
  Thomas Jefferson, Notes on the State of Virginia, Query 17, 1782

First off, I wanted to state there are always exceptions to the rule. Socrates would often demand absolute definitions as in what something is always. I would argue with Socrates that few things are "always" something certain as there are always exceptions to the rule. In general, men are physically stronger than women. Are there strong women who are stronger than many men are? Absolutely, but this is an exception rather than the general rule.

When analyzing tolerance, the focus is not tolerating evil, but tolerance as it relates to diverse individuals and groups of people.

Tolerance is required for all people to have equal rights. Good comes in all races, nationalities, religions, sexes, ages, IQs, incomes, heights, widths, hair styles, etc. Tolerance becomes strong when diverse people come together for a common goal or good. Tolerance is a characteristic of an advanced society. When taking an agnostic approach to gaining knowledge about people of different backgrounds and nationalities it's amazing how much we all have in common.

It's important to learn about different cultures and people. We are fortunate to have television series today that explore food and culture of people all across the world. Weather, food and shelter are things we all have in common. The generous hospitality the hosts on networks such as the Travel Channel and the Food Network receive when in other countries is truly amazing. These experiences promote tolerance.

Cruel intolerance is a byproduct of ignorance. In this world, we still have a few primitive intolerant countries. The leaders of these countries desperately cling to barbaric past rituals and beliefs, which lead to despicable acts such as the extreme suppression of women, and the deaths of homosexuals. Often their brutality is a result of arrogance and hate rather than any religious doctrine. They often pervert their own religion to serve their own self interests, and are oppressively intolerant of social progress or modern thinking.

In my own life, I have become tolerant of religions that are intolerant of my own beliefs. This is not to say I've never engaged in heated religious debates, or that the intolerance didn't bother me. In the spirit of Lao Tzu, I have become tolerant of intolerant religious beliefs, thus religious tolerance is attained. I cannot achieve what I desire to achieve by attacking religion. I cannot expect religious people to be tolerant of my beliefs if I am intolerant of theirs.

Sun Tzu in the *Art of War* taught not to besiege walled cities as too much time and resources will be expended, and one's weapons will become dull. Arguing with religious people that they shouldn't be religious is akin to besieging a walled city. In this case, the weapons don't get dull, the conversations do. Those who are devout in their faith will not abandon their beliefs no matter what argument is presented. For the religious people that are good, as the vast majority of people are, I have learned to accept them as they are; not how I think they should be. I have accepted them for how they think, not how I think they should think. And besides, as long as someone is good, whatever religion they affiliate with, it neither picks my pocket nor breaks my leg. Be tolerant.

Kindness and Wickedness

"Kindness in words creates confidence. Kindness is thinking creates profoundness. Kindness in giving creates love."
– Lao Tzu (6th century B.C.)

When I was young, I spent a lot of time riding my bike. Once I became desperately lost, and it was getting late and getting dark. As cell phones hadn't been invented yet, I had to rely on the kindness of strangers to get back home. I asked a man for help, and he stopped everything he was doing to help me. He found a map to get directions, put my bike in his car and took me home. Most people are kind and kind acts happen every day.

For the most part, kind acts don't make the news. If the man who had helped me had been wicked, instead of kind, if he had abducted, assaulted or killed me instead of helping me; that would have made the news. There are over 300 million people in America and approx. 4 billion people in the world. The news is filled with the wicked people who do the most despicable acts. The constant onslaught of bad news can be depressing, and cause families to raise their children in fear rather than faith. A constant barrage of despicable acts in the media promotes isolation. It's important to remember and have faith that the vast majority of people are kind. Kindness does not catch media attention day by day but does become newsworthy in the face of tragedies. People come together when disaster strikes to give time and money to strangers in need. Be kind.

Contentment and Greed

"Riches are not from an abundance of wordly goods, but from a contented mind." – Prophet Muhammad (570-632)

Some people will never have enough. When asked the question how much more do you need the answer will always be just a little more.

Recently there was a billionaire caught for insider trading. Although a billionaire, this person was involved with petty deceitful tactics to make a few thousand dollars more. These days there is a lot of talk about living beyond one's means due to the recent housing and economic downturn. There is a big difference between someone living beyond their means in a 1,000 sq. ft. house, and someone living beyond their means in a 10,000 sq. ft. house. There is a big difference between someone living beyond their means to have a home that is less than an hour away from their job, and someone living beyond their means to have an expensive vacation home they visit once or twice per year.

After an economic downturn, many of the people who lived lavishly regret not spending their money more wisely. On the flip side, many times people regret not taking a vacation when they had the chance. I knew a man who was married to the love of his life for 10 years. They never went on vacation and just kept trying to save money. His wife became ill and passed away. He now regrets being frugal those many years. The people who can never have enough will never be happy. The people who are content with what they have are happy. It's nice to buy nice things, but it's also nice to be financially secure. Finding the right balance takes wisdom. Of course there are many things in this world that money cannot buy that can make one content.

We must recognize the over-the-top greedy people who will never have enough and do what we can to keep them out of high government and business positions. One who cannot handle their own finances has no business in a high government position handling enormous budgets of taxpayer dollars. Someone who is extremely greedy is also far more corruptible. There can be extreme greed and there can be extreme contentment. I believe that making money and spending money on goods and services in a strong economic capitalistic society is a great way to live. Just don't spend too much money if you can help it. A little greed can be good, but ultimately it is in contentment that we should strive for, as that will lead to a happier life. Be content.

Respect and Jealousy

"The quickest way to a man's heart is through his chest."
– Roseanne Barr

Ptolemy of Mauretania was son to Anthony and Cleopatra. The Roman emperor Caligula invited him to Rome. Upon arrival Ptolemy wore a beautiful custom made purple cloak. Caligula was jealous of this purple cloak and had Ptolemy murdered so that he could have it.

The Greek Goddess Hera was the wife of Zeus. She was extremely jealous of his infidelities. She cast cruel punishment on the other women and their children. It was Hera who sent two serpents to kill Hercules, who was born from Zeus's affair with Alcmene.

Respect and jealousy are very powerful forces. Everyone wants respect. Many people wrongly believe that wealthy people and celebrities don't care about respect. When insulted, they just laugh all the way to the bank. This is not true. We are all human and all hurt when not treated with a certain level of respect. When someone who is blatantly disrespected claims that they don't care, or it doesn't matter, it's not true. It does matter, and it matters a lot.

Disrespect and jealousy have the ability to do great harm. They can bring out the worst in people. Jealousy happens when someone wants something someone else has. Jealousy is most intense when it comes to affection rather than something physical like a diamond. It's more potent when in regard to people, not things. Someone jealous of another's spouse is more dangerous than someone jealous of another's car.

Jealousy is directly related to greed. If one is content then one is not jealous. Respect is disserved to everyone initially. Confucius taught one should have respect for elders and believed in a structure of respect in society for men, women and children. When we know someone who has more than we, are we jealous or do we respect them? Of course we should know what more means. Does it mean more money, better looks, a better job, or nicer car? Does it mean they are with someone we want to be with? When faced with jealously believe in karma and contentment. Be respectful.

Integrity and Dishonesty

Quality in business needs to be an obsession. One mistake in quality can lead to a lost customer for life. Many car companies today are still suffering from bad quality experienced decades ago. People have long memories when they feel that they've been cheated. One can have a hamburger every day for years. One day they get a bad burger and the next day they're eating subs.

The word for quality in people is integrity. When someone has high integrity it means they are reliable to do the right thing every time. When someone is dishonest they can't be trusted. The people entrusted to have the highest level of integrity are people in public office. These people are expected to be the pillars of the community. Their reliability, professionalism and ethics are to be a standard for businesses and the public. When people in high public office and corporate positions are dishonest it sets a bad example for everyone. It is a betrayal of the common trust.

Be obsessed with maintaining your own integrity. Be the rock your family, coworkers and community can always rely on. Be the moral compass. Be the pillar. Have integrity.

> "Watch your thoughts; they become words. Watch your words; they become actions. Watch your actions; they become habits. Watch your habits; they become character. Watch your character; it becomes your destiny."   – Unknown Source

Does the definition of someone good mean someone with good characteristics? Does the definition of someone evil mean someone with evil or bad characteristics? We should all strive to have good character, but ultimately it is actions that dictate who someone is. Someone who does good is good, and someone who does evil is evil. This is my bias, and other philosophers or religious leaders might disagree stating evil must not exist in the heart or the actions. Philosophers such as Aristotle appear to agree with me. "Every rascal is not a thief, but every thief is a rascal." – Aristotle (384-322 B.C.)

This is a quote from the Prophet Muhammad, "'Who is the best man?' Muhammad replied, 'He is the best man whose life is long and whose actions are good.' 'Then who is the worst man?' 'He whose life is long and whose actions are bad." – Prophet Muhammad (570-632)

Religions differ on ways of explaining and addressing good and evil but one thing is clear, good and evil are recognized and do exist. Are good and evil normal occurrences in nature? These are natural occurrences in evolutions' survival of the fittest perhaps? If life is designed and created, why did the creation include both good and evil?

Time for some additional perspective by the opposing views of Socrates and Machiavelli. Is man generally good but corruptible by the evils of society? Is man generally evil and needs a law abiding society in order for him to be good?

Socrates taught that "there is only one good -- knowledge; and only one evil -- ignorance." He also taught "knowledge is virtue, ignorance is vice." What does this mean? Basically, someone who does evil is dumb. They believe doing evil things will make them happy, but it never does. If they would be enlightened to the fact only doing good things would make them happy then they would only do good deeds.

Niccolo Machiavelli (1469-1527) famous for his work *The Prince* and his quote, ""the end justifies the means" had a different interpretation of good and evil. Socrates believed that men were innately good. Machiavelli believed men were innately evil. Some of Machiavelli's quotes include:

- "Of mankind we may say in general they are fickle, hypocritical, and greedy of gain."
- "The fact is that a man who wants to act virtuously in every way necessarily comes to grief among so many who are not virtuous."
- "Where the willingness is great, the difficulties cannot be great."
- "There is no avoiding war; it can only be postponed to the advantage of others."
- "Ambition is so powerful a passion in the human breast, that however high we reach we are never satisfied."

When it came to politics and government Plato believed the goal was ethics. Machiavelli argued that ethics were not realistic and that the goal was prosperous survival at all costs. The following quotes reflect his belief:

- "Many have dreamed up republics and principalities that have never in truth been known to exist; the gulf between how one should live and how one does live is so wide that a man who neglects what is actually done for what should be done learns the way to self-destruction rather than self-preservation."

- "Since it is difficult to join them together, it is safer to be feared than to be loved when one of the two must be lacking."
- "A prince never lacks legitimate reasons to break his promise."

Is mankind generally evil, and needs a law abiding society in order for him to be good? Machiavelli would argue yes. Good arms are required for men to do good. "The main foundations of every state, new states as well as ancient or composite ones, are good laws and good arms you cannot have good laws without good arms, and where there are good arms, good laws inevitably follow."

The similarities of philosophers in different periods of time can be quite remarkable. It appears Machiavelli's views of man differ from those of Socrates and Plato but what about Aristotle? The following quote may surprise you. "At his best, man is the noblest of all animals; separated from law and justice his is the worst." – Aristotle (384-322 B.C.)

Was Machiavelli a "might makes right" preacher, or simply a political pragmatist? Must one be as ruthless as ones' enemies if not more so in order to survive? One must be aware of the time in which these philosophers are writing. Machiavelli wrote in a time of war, and knew the history of war which is filled with the rise and fall of military powers of one country after another. Does war harden the heart? Socrates was a soldier in times of conflict, but he did not take the utilitarian stance of Machiavelli. Socrates; however, was not arrested and tortured for conspiracy as Machiavelli was in his lifetime. Dramatic lifetime events can have profound impact on our perception of humanity. It certainly did for Plato when Socrates was sentenced to death.

In the philosophical battle between Socrates and Machiavelli who is right? There are approx. 2,000 years between the birth of Socrates (469 B.C.) and Machiavelli (1469 A.D.). During this time and even hundreds of years later it has overwhelmingly been a Machiavelli world. For the most part, leaders have not acted on ethics; they have acted on greed and preservation. The Roman conquests were not ethical, they were brutal. A Roman army that performed poorly in a battle would often be decimated. One out of every ten soldiers would be cut down as punishment. How do you defend against a force this blood thirsty, brutal and ruthless? Must you compromise ethical principles in order to survive?

The battle is not over yet. It appears Socrates and his followers ultimately failed based on actions to raise the morality of the ancient Greeks and other countries. Perhaps they were simply ahead of the brutal times they were living in. Sometimes change takes a great deal of time, and often battles need to be fought continually in order to be won.

I'm going to take a slight detour from the good and evil debate to discuss Eastern philosophers, specifically Confucius and Lao Tzu. It's important to note Western civilization does not have the monopoly on ancient philosophical teachings of morality and ethics that promote goodness. In Eastern civilization, philosophers such as Confucius and Lao Tzu also taught morality, ethics and wisdom.

Amazing similarities between Confucius to Socrates can be found in the following quote. "To know is to know that you know nothing. That is the meaning of true knowledge." – Confucius (551-479B.C.). The widely known English translation of the Golden Rule in the New Testament Luke 6:31 is, "Do unto other as you would have them do unto you." Confucius wrote something very similar approx. 500 years earlier, "What you do not want others to do to you, do not do to others."

Please pardon the additional side note about Confucius, but I'm sure the big question going through your mind right now is how the philosophy of Confucius compares with legendary American military commander George S. Patton and legendary American football coach Vince Lombardi. I'm joking of course, although the following quotes may surprise you.

- "Our greatest glory is not in never failing, but in rising every time we fall." – Confucius (551-479B.C.)
- "I don't measure a man's success by how high he climbs but how high he bounces when he hits bottom." – George S. Patton (1885-1945)
- "It's not whether you get knocked down, it's whether you get up." – Vince Lombardi (1913-1970)

Socrates taught justice must apply to enemies as it does to everyone.

Jesus preached tolerance and even love for enemies. There is no one who more elegantly explains this wisdom than Lao Tzu in his quote, "Treat those who are good with goodness, and also treat those who are not good with goodness. Thus goodness is attained. Be honest to those who are honest, and be also honest to those who are not honest. Thus honesty is attained." – Lao Tzu (6th century B.C.)

Good is ethical, evil is unethical. Good is moral, evil is immoral. Evil will never be destroyed. Good will never surrender. The fight of good against evil will continue through the end of mankind. Will we have a renaissance of ancient Eastern and Western ethical teachings? Is the world ripe for such a movement or has this already been occurring in the background for quite some time? What has the great experiment known as United States of America taught us? Despite the bad news we are seemingly inundated with every day, in many ways humanity has made remarkable moral advancements in the world. Great battles have been won over slavery and oppression. Currently, our politics and society are not primarily focused on ethics, but the potential is there.

- "Feed the hungry and visit a sick person, and free the captive, if he be unjustly confined. Assist any person oppressed, whether Muslim or non-Muslim." – Prophet Muhammad (570-632)
- "Darkness cannot drive out darkness; only light can do that. Hate cannot drive out hate; only love can do that." – Martin Luther King Jr. (1929-1968)

The Worst of Evil:
- Butchering unarmed men, women and children
- Destroying history
- Convicting innocent people and sentencing them to pain and death
- Taking a widows' land by accusing her of being a witch and having her burned at the stake.
- Purposely spreading disease to innocent people by giving them infected blankets and clothing
- Using people like property
- Forcing people to live in fear
- Rape
- Oppressing women and minorities

- Torturing and murdering people for having different beliefs
- Torturing and murdering animals for personal amusement or gain
- Torturing and recklessly murdering people in the name of religion or country
- Stealing retirement and savings from dedicated workers
- Denying opportunity to others that one had himself

The Best of Good:

- Protecting unarmed men, women and children
- Preserving history
- Protecting all people from unjust trial and punishment
- Protecting people from cruel laws and customs
- Curing disease
- Maintaining justice over perverted religious injustice
- Banning slavery and fighting human trafficking
- Allowing people to live free and in peace
- Protecting women and children from sexual predators
- Promoting equal rights
- Tolerance of different beliefs
- Protecting animals from those who would hurt them for amusement or personal gain
- Helping people in the name of religion or country
- Protecting the savings and retirement of workers from corporate thieves and fools
- Grant, promote and expand the opportunities of your generation to the next generation

Be Good

EVOLUTION VS. CREATIONISM
AND OLD EARTH VS. NEW EARTH

An agnostic approach is ideal for adding perspective to ongoing arguments. Both sides are analyzed from a neutral perspective initially. The mind is cleared of preconceived notions and knowledge is built from the ground up on a solid foundation. An open minded and broad range of perspective is used to identify fresh and unique angles to the problem that may result in a solution. Evolution vs. creationism has been an argument since Charles Darwin published *Origin of Species*. Old Earth vs. new Earth theory is a recent dispute which may not be with us for long.

Creationism has become a Christian expression to argue against evolution and develop theories that coincide with biblical scripture. This is unfortunate as creationism and intelligent design should be legitimate scientific study rather than terms that merely serve a specific religious agenda. There was a recent survey that posed the question, "Do you believe in evolution?" It's really not that simple. One can believe in certain aspects of evolution but disagree with Charles Darwin on others. Evolution has a stigma of being anti-religious and somehow a direct contradiction to religious theories on life. I don't believe this is accurate. Mr. Darwin's book was *The Origin of Species* not the Origin of Life. Darwin never explains the origin of life, nor was he an atheist. Darwin and his protective friend Thomas H. Huxley were agnostics. As stated earlier, Huxley is the one who created the term agnostic.

If you believe certain characteristics of a species can change due to changes in habitat over long periods of time, then you believe in one aspect of evolution. For example, if a specific species' habitat changes from shade to sunlight, you might expect pigmentation of the skin to change in order to better deal with sunlight, and a possible thickening of the skin in certain areas to deal with heat, such as traveling on hot sand or rock. Evolution works through survival of the fittest and selective breeding to promote specific characteristics of future generations, causing the species to gradually change over time.

A basic example of this evolution is turtles on an island during a drought. The turtles with longer necks are able to survive as they can reach the food. The turtles with short necks die out. The resulting generations of turtles have longer necks. Perhaps as survival instinct the female turtles now have an attraction to males with the longest necks or vice versa. Selective breeding also promotes certain attributes of the species. The main requirement in this example would be for the turtles to have various neck lengths that would be significant enough for some to reach food over others. What about the turtles that build ladders to go up and get the food? All kidding aside, I don't believe this idea of evolution is farfetched or unreasonable, and is actually, in fact, proven; however, it comes far short of explaining everything.

William Paley (1743-1805) argued that life is intelligently designed and must have a creator. He used an example of finding a watch on a beach. The watch has intricate components placed together with a purpose. It is not something of chance and when studying a watch one realizes it must have had a creator. Like the watch, life has complex intricate components that are fitted together to serve a purpose. In regard to complexity, living organisms are more complex than watches as Paley would say, "in a degree which exceeds all computation." Paley's argument would be this is not by chance, but rather by design.

Darwin's theory of evolution was much inspired by his visits to the Galapagos Islands. These islands 600 miles away from South America contained unique animal species and breeds found nowhere else. Many species resembled those in South America and likely originated from there, but after time isolated on the islands (which rose from the sea due to volcanic activity) had changed. A noticeable trait supporting evolutionary theory is the shape of a bird's beak to feed on the variety of food specific to the area they live in.

So let's say the variety of animal breeds only found on the Galapagos Islands proves evolution as minor changes in species' attributes over time. The development of a bird's beak is insignificant in comparison to the creation of the eye. There are attributes that are unique to the species and breeds that exist only in the Galapagos Islands; however, there are far more attributes that are the same. You don't find species with a third eye or extra arm. You don't find species with un-natural attributes or abilities. There are currently many varieties of dog breeds from Chihuahuas to bull mastiffs, but they are all canines. They are all still dogs. They are all still the same species with many common characteristics.

William Paley argues that an examination of the eye is in itself a cure for atheism. Could the eye be created by evolution? Would a logical assumption be the eye could only be created by an entity that already sees or has the concept of sight? What does the evidence suggest? Fossil evidence is required for the obtainment of truth between creationism and evolution.

Fossil evidence does reveal transitional periods of species proving evolution in the sense of certain attributes changing over time is true. Fossil evidence also reveals life has existed on Earth for billions of years. Through studying fossils from certain periods of history one can trace a species over time and compare the common attributes of ancestors and record changes. Changes can include the movement of features such as the nostril, reduction in toes, disappearance of claws that once existed at the end of wings, disappearance of legs on snakes, disappearance of teeth on whales, etc. Studying fossils can show common attributes between species such as bone structures and possible lineages to a common ancestor. All dogs can be traced back to a common ancestral wolf.

Not all evolutionary theory is explained by fossil evidence. Fossil records show animals appearing and disappearing without any transitional period or trace of an ancestor or descendant. Giraffe fossils have been found without any transitional evidence for the evolution of the long neck. It appears at one time giraffes didn't exist, and then all the sudden they were here. In periods of history there have been explosions of new species. We don't know why. There is evidence of sudden massive amounts of new species without evidence of mass evolution. There are also species that go unchanged over great amounts of time.

I believe that certain attributes in species can change in time based on survival of the fittest, changes in environment, and selective breeding. Darwin maintained that species can evolve into different species. There is no direct evidence of this. All the different breeds of dogs are all dogs. There is no breed of dog that is something different than a dog. In history where new species appeared, where did they come from? Were they born from other animals? The common theory is species cannot interbreed with each other as their reproductive systems are different. Is this theory really true? How much do we really know about interbreeding among different species? Were new species placed on Earth as one would place new fish in an aquarium? We don't know. And all of these theories still do not explain the origin of life. Something has to exist in order to evolve.

Let's suppose Darwin is right and species can evolve from other species. Evolution is a great tree of life where the branches represent species and they all come from a common trunk. There are branches off of other branches as species branched out from other species. The tree of life is incomprehensibly large and complex. Imagine the seed this tree grew from.

Let's suppose creationism is right, and a greater being placed different species of life on Earth. According to fossil records, life was not placed on Earth all at once. Different species of life were placed on Earth in phases.

Sometimes finding the truth is like herding cats. Nothing should be simply dismissed without some investigation when using the agnostic approach. Not even astrology (which is the father of astronomy and has existed for thousands of years) should be completely dismissed as a false theory of personalities and fortune telling without some investigation. According to our scientific disciplines of biology and astronomy the Earth is approx. 4.6 billion years old and life has existed for approx. 3 billion years. There is a young Earth theory that places the Earth at 6,000 years old. Is this real science or simply an attempt to prove Old Testament biblical scripture? The age of 6,000 years comes from the biblical Genesis days actually being our 24-hour days and a biblical scholarly estimate of 4,000 years between the first man Adam and Jesus Christ. Add the 2,000 years since Jesus and you get 6,000.

At first glance, the young Earth theory appears plausible. The arguments are if the Earth was billions of years old the oceans would have more sentiment, the moon would have more dust, the Earth's magnetic field would have been too strong in the past, Jupiter would be cooler and the Moon would have floated away by now. All these arguments have been scientifically countered as not accurate measurements of time (http://www.talkorigins.org/faqs/faq-age-of-earth.html.) Of all the methods used to measure the age of the Earth, the evidence supporting an old Earth are overwhelming. Methods include evidence from layers of rock, erosion, and layers of ice. Three scientific dating methods include:

- *Radio Carbon Dating* – Used to measure the age of organic material such as wood and bone. Carbon has three isotopes. Two isotopes are stable but Carbon 14 decays at a very slow rate with a half life of approximately 5,700 years.
- *Potassium-argon Dating* – Used to measure the age of igneous rocks. Potassium-40 decays to Argon-40 at a very slow rate with a half life of 1.3 billion years.
- *Rubidium-strontium Dating* – Used to measure the age of mineral and rock. Rubidium-87 decays to Strontium-87 at a very slow rate with a half life of approx. 48.8 billion years.

We can also measure the age of the Sun and the stars by dissecting light. Our sun generates heat through nuclear fusion. The outward push of nuclear fusion and inward pull of gravity are fortunately equalized and stable. Through nuclear fusion the stars are converting hydrogen into the heaver element helium. By measuring the hydrogen to helium composition, we can measure the age of the stars. Our Sun is estimated to be 4.6 billion years old with a life expectancy of 10 billion years.

My agnostic conclusion is that the Earth and life are far older than 6,000 years. The dating methods do have a percentage of error; however, the sheer differences between 4,600,000,000 and 6,000 are, shall we say, just a wee bit beyond that percentage. The Egyptians didn't build the pyramids within a few hundred years of the great flood in the Old Testament which young Earth proponents are claiming was merely 5,000 years ago. Imagine the established society, strong central government, language, experience, foundation of mathematics, architecture and skilled craftsmen required to build the Great Pyramids. Remember, this was accomplished approx. 4,500 years ago from today and approx. 1,500 years before Moses and Ramses the Great. There are also Egyptian relics that are far older than the earliest pyramids.

So does old Earth disprove Christianity? It does not. Christians have explained how old Earth coincides with the Bible. Explanations include the days in Genesis actually being great periods of time rather than the 24-hour day. Another explanation is a large period of time existing between Genesis 1:1 and Genesis 1:2. In a logical way, this makes sense as the 24-hour day based on the Earth's rotation did not exist before the Earth was created. How could a 24-hour day be a unit of measurement before days existed? What is a day to a God?

When using an agnostic approach one often finds truth on both sides. Based on my research and philosophizing there is clear evidence of evolution in regard to species changing over time. There is no concrete evidence that supports species evolving into other species. There are also serious questions as to what evolution can accomplish, and what it cannot. Can eyes evolve into existence without the concept of sight? Can wings evolve into existence without the concept of flying? I believe there is clear evidence of intelligent design and once again, this concept should be legitimate scientific study and not part of any religious agenda. So when faced with the question, "Do you believe in evolution?" I'm not quite sure how to answer. It's not a yes or no question, unless the definition is further defined. In regard to old Earth vs. new Earth the evidence is clear. The Earth is very old.

WHAT WE KNOW – FOUR EXAMPLES

What do we know is absolutely true? Some philosophers deny that anything is real. These would be the "life is all just a great illusion" people. For the sake of practicality and sanity, I will maintain that our lives are very much real. Four examples of what we know are:

- *There has always been something*
- *The Physical Universe*
- *The Biological Universe*
- *The Universal Will*

There is no point in time where nothing existed. There has always been something. The premise for this theory is simple. You cannot get something out of nothing. Mathematically the argument would go like this. $0=0$. If $0=X$ then $X=0$. $X+0=0$. X multiplied or divided by zero is zero. The square root of zero is zero. It's a purely logical conclusion. Just as evolution needs an origin of life as something needs to exist in order to evolve the same holds true for the Universe. Something has always existed that has resulted in the Universe we live in and observe today and the Universe that exists beyond our senses.

The physical universe consists of the stars, planets and the moons. The physical universe is immense with billions and billions of stars and galaxies. The universe consists of materials that are represented in the Periodic Table of Elements. This table lists 118 elements that range from metals, non-metals, solids, liquids, gases and other substances with unknown characteristics. This table can be found at www.ptable.com.

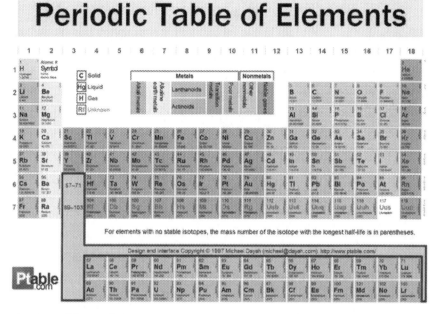

(www.ptable.com)

The physical world can exist with or without the biological world. The biological world requires the physical world in order to exist. On Earth, the biological world consists of over 375,000 species of plants, 1,000,000 species of insects, 20,000 species of fish, 6,000 species of reptiles, 9,000 species of birds, 1,000 species of amphibians, and 15,000 species of mammals.

Life is made up of the same elements as the stars and planets. The differences being these elements are organized in a way to enable voluntary movement and intelligence. The difference is amazingly complex and miraculous. Another note, the biologists who study life tend to be more religious than the astronomers who study stars. There appears to be more signs of God in the biological universe than in the physical universe.

But wait! There's more! So if we organize carbon, hydrogen, nitrogen, oxygen, phosphorus and sulfur in the right way to enable voluntary movement we now have life right? Wrong! Life needs to have motivation including the willpower to live and multiply. The most primitive internal functions required for life such as eating and breathing also require intelligence to exist. Without willpower the organism dies. It would be stuck in neutral. The lights are on, but nobodies home. Why does life want to live and multiply? Why does life evolve? I would call this the universal will. What is the purpose of mankind? To survive and multiply is our purpose. Is that the only purpose? That is the question.

IS HISTORY ACCURATE?

An agnostic needs to gather and validate facts carefully. Most of our knowledge can be found in history; however, is history a trusted source for knowledge? Often deciphering history can be challenging. We are blessed to have an abundance of well preserved ancient Egyptian history; however, historians did have a challenge to overcome. The ancient Egyptians didn't believe in recording bad news. Historians had to find other ways to get an accurate account of the past. In ancient Egyptian history one could tell when a war was going badly as the recorded victories would come closer and closer to the capitol city. One could tell when the economy was bad when the tombs of pharaohs were less splendid. One could tell there was unrest when the pharaohs changed often.

History is often written by the victors who are not likely to give their enemies a fair portrayal. History can also be rewritten over time. People who study this phenomenon analyze older written text such as antique elementary school history books and compare them to new text. The differences between the two are then analyzed to find out what was changed, when it was changed and possibly why. "Under God" was not in the original version, but added to the Pledge of Allegiance in 1954 by Congress. Columbus did not discover the world was round as I was taught in school. This knowledge came long before Columbus.

The ancient Egyptians sometimes rewrote history, which was difficult as much of their history was literally written in stone. One could tell when rewriting took place as some impressions in the stone would be deeper than others. For example, Hatshepsut was by all accounts a great Egyptian pharaoh. Egypt thrived under the rule of Hatshepsut for approx. 15 years. The problem was Hatshepsut was a woman. Egypt was the most tradition conservative nation ever and traditionally all pharaohs were men. The successor of Hatshepsut had the records of her as pharaoh erased. Not everything was erased, so we can conclude the purpose was not to eliminate the great female pharaoh from history, just the record of her ruling as pharaoh.

So where does history begin? History begins with writing. Long before writing, drawings and paintings were created. The earliest cave paintings are estimated to be over 25,000 years old. Before writing, oral language was developed. Anything recorded generation to generation was done so orally through stories.

This Egyptian carving uses syllabic figures as alphabet. These stone tablets tell us of Nar-Mer who united Upper and Lower Egypt approx.

3,100 B.C. Nar-Mer ruled Egypt before the Great Pyramids of Giza were built, which began under the pharaoh Khufu who ruled 2589-2566 B.C. in the 4th dynasty.

The history and development of language is a complex study in itself. One can find similarity in words that exist in different cultures that give clues to origins and lineage of languages.

How much have ancient stories that originated from long past ancestors changed from the beginning until the time they were actually written down? It's hard to tell. Often stories do get bigger and bigger as they are told over and over again. History did not begin at the same time across all countries as writing did not begin at the same time across all countries. Some countries have earlier historical records than others. Much history has also been destroyed during the ages by neglect and war.

History has been edited and much has been left out. History was written by people and therefore, contains interpretation and bias from the people that wrote it. History has often been distorted and sugar coated in an attempt to suppress guilt and anger. Should people feel guilty when other people of the same race were victimized or committed atrocities in the past? Should not people feel proud of the good people in the past that fought for what was right? For every villain that brings shame and despair, there is a hero that brings pride and hope. In the worst of times there have always been people who challenged injustice and faced torture and death for helping others. So is history accurate? Not completely and much of it is open to interpretation.

Historians are trained experts at deciphering history. They use a scientific approach utilizing selective criteria in order to determine if something actually happened the way it was written. Historians have been able to accurately reconstruct many historical events. Many historians today such as Professor James W. Loewen are on a mission to correct distorted historical events currently taught in our schools. I applaud their efforts. We all have a right to know the truth regarding the past. Watered down history has caused a great disinterest in our society for this important study. True history is far more interesting and engaging.

The United States of America has a long history for such a young nation. Many unspeakable crimes against humanity have been committed by Americans. You will not find most of these atrocities in the history books. Many generous acts of kindness and compassion have been committed by Americans. In American history there have been many heroes and many villains. So what does history tell us about America?

Is America a nation that is good, or a nation that is evil according to history? This question is subjective. If ones' goal is to portray America as evil, they will find historical evidence to make their case. If ones' goal is to portray America as good, they will find historical evidence to make their case. Personally, I believe there is more historical good than evil in America. I believe America is, for the most part, a good ethical society.

Does America have the potential to be significantly better than it is today? The answer would be absolutely. Does America have the potential to be worse than it is today? The answer would also be absolutely. I would argue that America is good as it was built on a moral and ethical foundation and morally and ethically the potential to be worse is exponentially greater than the potential to be better. To be fair, many of the great advancements of morality and ethics in America are recent. To find unspeakable oppression of minorities, one only needs to look back a hundred years.

So what is the conclusion about history? It's important to know the past, so we don't repeat the same mistakes, and to know the circumstances and reasoning that shaped the world as we live in now. It's also important to know historical realities such as history was written by people through their own interpretation and bias. Sometimes history was also rewritten due to many reasons, including the manipulation of historical occurrences for personal gain by people in power. History is important; however, we must be more mindful of the present and the future. We must learn from the past, but we cannot live in the past.

"Change is the law of life. And those who look only to the past or present are certain to miss the future."
— John F. Kennedy (1917-1963)

FREEDOM AND QUALITY OF LIFE

"Freedom is never more than one generation away from extinction. We didn't pass it to our children in the bloodstream. It must be fought for, protected, and handed on for them to do the same."   – Ronald Reagan (1911-2004)

Could you image being jailed and tortured for having an opinion? The Italian scientist Galileo Galilei (1564-1642) supported the views of astronomer Nicolas Copernicus (1473-1543) that the universe did not revolve around the Earth. Copernicus had this crazy heliocentric theory, which defied thousands of years of traditional views, that somehow the Sun was the center of our solar system. Galileo built telescopes and studied the moons of Jupiter. If everything revolved around the Earth, how was it possible moons were orbiting Jupiter?

Well so what? Galileo has freedom of speech and is entitled to any view or opinion he wants to make, right? Well, not exactly. The US concept of freedom of speech didn't exist yet. The church declared any opinions that differed from the Earth being the center of the universe as heresy. Galileo was brought before the Inquisition in 1616, and was given the choice of either recanting his opinion or face medieval torture. Not surprisingly, Galileo recanted and then spent his final years under house arrest.

Without historical context, freedom is largely unappreciated. Freedom is about having options and protection. One is not free to hurt others; one is free from harm in what they do and who they are.

I would like to redefine freedom as Socrates redefined justice. Many people in this country believe freedom as merely the right to vote. This I believe is a very short sighted view of freedom and needs to be expanded. Freedom in the past was far more associated with slavery than it is today. For the most part, we have defeated slavery and now need to elevate the definition of freedom as more than not being someone else's personal property.

Abraham Maslow (1908-1970) was a psychologist who studied human needs for motivation. He developed what today is called Maslow's Hierarchy of Needs. At the bottom of the hierarchy are the most basic needs; at the top are the most advanced. I will discuss freedom and quality of life as it relates to Maslow's work. I will not be discussing freedom is it relates to people with disabilities here, but it is important to note that disabilities do cause great losses of individual freedom.

Maslow's Hierarchy of Needs includes:

Self-actualization – Morality, creativity, spontaneity, problem solving, lack of prejudice, acceptance of facts

Esteem – Self-esteem, confidence, achievement, respect of others, respect by others

Love/ Belonging – Friendship, family, sexual intimacy

Safety – Security of body, of employment, of resources, or morality, of the family, of health, of property

Physiological – Breathing, food, water, sex, sleep, homeostasis, excretion

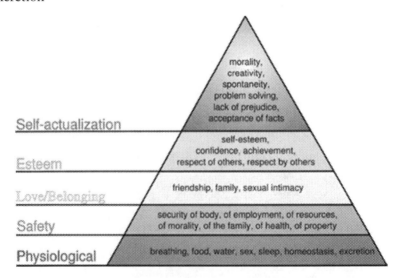

At the beginning of the hierarchy, we have breathing, food, water, sex, sleep, homeostasis and excretion. In this sense sex is our primitive urge to have sex for survival, not related to love and belonging. As you can see sex is repeated as sexual intimacy under love/ belonging higher up in the hierarchy. I understand why Maslow has sex listed under the most basic needs but at the same time sexual needs vary greatly among people. Not everyone needs to have sex, but all people need to eat and drink. Homeostasis simply means the body is functioning like it's supposed to such as keeping core temperature, blood flow, etc.

Breathing is too basic, so let's begin with food and how that is related to freedom. For the purposes of this exercise food will also include drink.

No Freedom	One is in starvation and will eat or drink the first available substance that can be kept down in order to survive be it a bug, a dirty puddle or garbage.
Some Freedom	A staple food is always available such as rice, bread or potatoes but no variety.
More Freedom	A staple food is always available, and once a week you can also eat a bit of beef and fruit.
Ultimate Freedom	One has the means to obtain food from any culture or part of the world. One can have fresh vegetables and fruit of any variety, any kind of meat or fish, any kind of dairy, bread, pastry, any kind of spices or herbs, any kind of cooking style, any kind of drink such as fine wines and ales. Any cuisine is immediately available at any time such as French, Italian, Indian, German, Swedish, Russian, Pakistani, Chinese, African, American, etc.

The second level of the pyramid is Safety. This includes security of body, of employment, of resources, of morality, of the family, of health, of property. In the US, many of these needs are provided by law, they are your rights. The one crucial need that is not provided by law is the security of employment. Everybody needs to work and without an income you are at great risk of not achieving Maslow's advanced needs such as safety, love/ belonging, esteem and self actualization. It is crucial in any industrial society that the opportunity to work is available to all willing to take it. Without jobs, industrial societies suffer greatly at every level through unemployment, poverty and crime.

What is freedom in regard to employment?

No Freedom	No jobs, no employment
Some Freedom	An occasional temporary job that brings in a little money
More Freedom	Jobs are available through the private sector and government sponsored programs that ensure anyone seeking employment can be put to work immediately.
Ultimate Freedom	Your skills and talents are desperately sought after by the private sector. Companies are begging you to work for them. You can get a well paying job with excellent benefits instantly, in any part of the world, at any time. With job security, you have the means to achieve all the basic and advanced needs in Maslow's pyramid.

Is the previous analysis in regard to freedom or opportunity? They are directly related. In life, you will have opportunities to better yourself and others. Always take the opportunity to enable more freedom. If you have the opportunity to better your skills in the job market then take it. That opportunity will lead to greater freedom.

What does freedom mean in the United States of America? Before the US was formed, there were monarchies with no individual freedoms for the people. Individuals had no rights. The king and the church had power to oppress anyone and everyone. Today, American citizens have the Bill of Rights, which includes ten amendments and was established in 1791, a few years after the US Constitution was ratified in 1787. These amendments include individual rights such as freedom of speech, freedom to bear arms, freedom of religion and freedom from cruel and unusual punishment. The ten amendments that make up the

Bill of Rights were later expanded as amendments 11-27 were added. Expanded Amendments include:

- Amendment 13 passed in 1865 bans slavery
- Amendment 15 passed in 1869 bans the denial of voting rights to people based on race or color.
- Amendment 16 passed in 1909 began income tax (not all amendments are in regard to individual rights)
- Amendment 18 passed in 1917 bans alcohol
- Amendment 21 passed in 1933 repeals Amendment 18 (for sixteen years, alcohol was illegal in the US)
- Amendment 19 passed in 1919 bans the denial of voting rights to women.
- Amendment 22 passed in 1947 allows the President of the United States to serve no more than two terms.

Below are the original ten amendments of the United States Bill of Rights, and amendments 11-27. This was obtained from http://www.billofrights.org and http://www.archives.gov/exhibits/charters/constitution_amendments_11-27.html.

The Bill of Rights

The First 10 Amendments to the
Constitution as Ratified by the States
December 15, 1791

Preamble

Congress OF THE United States

begun and held at the City of New York, on Wednesday
the Fourth of March, one thousand seven hundred and eighty nine.

THE Conventions of a number of the States having at the time of their adopting the Constitution, expressed a desire, in order to prevent misconstruction or abuse of its powers, that further declaratory and restrictive clauses should be added: And as extending the ground of public confidence in the Government, will best insure the beneficent ends of its institution

RESOLVED by the Senate and House of Representatives of the United States of America, in Congress assembled, two thirds of both Houses concurring, that the following Articles be proposed to the Legislatures of the several States, as Amendments to the Constitution of the United States, all or any of which Articles, when ratified by three fourths of the said Legislatures, to be valid to all intents and purposes, as part of the said Constitution; viz.:

ARTICLES in addition to, and Amendment of the Constitution of the United States of America, proposed by Congress, and ratified by the Legislatures of the several States, pursuant to the fifth Article of the original Constitution.

Amendment I

Congress shall make no law respecting an establishment of religion, or prohibiting the free exercise thereof; or abridging the freedom of speech, or of the press; or the right of the people peaceably to assemble, and to petition the Government for a redress of grievances.

Amendment II

A well regulated Militia being necessary to the security of a free State, the right of the people to keep and bear Arms shall not be infringed.

Amendment III

No Soldier shall, in time of peace be quartered in any house, without the consent of the Owner, nor in time of war, but in a manner to be prescribed by law.

Amendment IV

The right of the people to be secure in their persons, houses, papers, and effects, against unreasonable searches and seizures, shall not be violated, and no Warrants shall issue, but upon probable cause, supported by Oath or affirmation, and particularly describing the place to be searched, and the persons or things to be seized.

Amendment V

No person shall be held to answer for a capital, or otherwise infamous crime, unless on a presentment or indictment of a Grand Jury, except in cases arising in the land or naval forces, or in the Militia, when in actual service in time of War or public danger; nor shall any person be subject for the same offence to be twice put in jeopardy of life or limb; nor shall be compelled in any criminal case to be a witness against himself, nor be deprived of life, liberty, or property, without due process of law; nor shall private property be taken for public use, without just compensation.

Amendment VI

In all criminal prosecutions, the accused shall enjoy the right to a speedy and public trial, by an impartial jury of the State and district wherein the crime shall have been committed, which district shall have been previously ascertained by law, and to be informed of the nature and cause of the accusation; to be confronted with the witnesses against him; to have compulsory process for obtaining witnesses in his favor, and to have the Assistance of Counsel for his defense.

Amendment VII

In suits at common law, where the value in controversy shall exceed twenty dollars, the right of trial by jury shall be preserved, and no fact tried by a jury, shall be otherwise reexamined in any Court of the United States, than according to the rules of the common law.

Amendment VIII

Excessive bail shall not be required, nor excessive fines imposed, nor cruel and unusual punishments inflicted.

Amendment IX

The enumeration in the Constitution, of certain rights, shall not be construed to deny or disparage others retained by the people.

Amendment X

The powers not delegated to the United States by the Constitution, nor prohibited by it to the States, are reserved to the States respectively, or to the people.

Amendment XI

Passed by Congress March 4, 1794. Ratified February 7, 1795.
Note: Article III, section 2, of the Constitution was modified by amendment 11.
The Judicial power of the United States shall not be construed to extend to any suit in law or equity, commenced or prosecuted against one of the United States by Citizens of another State, or by Citizens or Subjects of any Foreign State.

Amendment XII

Passed by Congress December 9, 1803. Ratified June 15, 1804.
Note: A portion of Article II, section 1 of the Constitution was superseded by the 12th amendment.
The Electors shall meet in their respective states and vote by ballot for President and Vice-President, one of whom, at least, shall not be an inhabitant of the same state with themselves; they shall name in their ballots the person voted for as President, and in distinct ballots the person voted for as Vice-President, and they shall make distinct lists of all persons voted for as President, and of all persons voted for as Vice-President, and of the number of votes for each, which lists they shall sign and certify,

and transmit sealed to the seat of the government of the United States, directed to the President of the Senate; -- the President of the Senate shall, in the presence of the Senate and House of Representatives, open all the certificates and the votes shall then be counted; -- The person having the greatest number of votes for President, shall be the President, if such number be a majority of the whole number of Electors appointed; and if no person have such majority, then from the persons having the highest numbers not exceeding three on the list of those voted for as President, the House of Representatives shall choose immediately, by ballot, the President. But in choosing the President, the votes shall be taken by states, the representation from each state having one vote; a quorum for this purpose shall consist of a member or members from two-thirds of the states, and a majority of all the states shall be necessary to a choice. [And if the House of Representatives shall not choose a President whenever the right of choice shall devolve upon them, before the fourth day of March next following, then the Vice-President shall act as President, as in case of the death or other constitutional disability of the President. --]* The person having the greatest number of votes as Vice-President, shall be the Vice-President, if such number be a majority of the whole number of Electors appointed, and if no person have a majority, then from the two highest numbers on the list, the Senate shall choose the Vice-President; a quorum for the purpose shall consist of two-thirds of the whole number of Senators, and a majority of the whole number shall be necessary to a choice. But no person constitutionally ineligible to the office of President shall be eligible to that of Vice-President of the United States.
Superseded by section 3 of the 20th amendment.

Amendment XIII
Passed by Congress January 31, 1865. Ratified December 6, 1865.
Note: A portion of Article IV, section 2, of the Constitution was superseded by the 13th amendment.
Section 1.
Neither slavery nor involuntary servitude, except as a punishment for crime whereof the party shall have been duly convicted, shall exist within the United States, or any place subject to their jurisdiction.
Section 2.
Congress shall have power to enforce this article by appropriate legislation.

Amendment XIV

Passed by Congress June 13, 1866. Ratified July 9, 1868.

Note: Article I, section 2, of the Constitution was modified by section 2 of the 14th amendment.

Section 1.

All persons born or naturalized in the United States, and subject to the jurisdiction thereof, are citizens of the United States and of the State wherein they reside. No State shall make or enforce any law which shall abridge the privileges or immunities of citizens of the United States; nor shall any State deprive any person of life, liberty, or property, without due process of law; nor deny to any person within its jurisdiction the equal protection of the laws.

Section 2.

Representatives shall be apportioned among the several States according to their respective numbers, counting the whole number of persons in each State, excluding Indians not taxed. But when the right to vote at any election for the choice of electors for President and Vice-President of the United States, Representatives in Congress, the Executive and Judicial officers of a State, or the members of the Legislature thereof, is denied to any of the male inhabitants of such State, being twenty-one years of age,* and citizens of the United States, or in any way abridged, except for participation in rebellion, or other crime, the basis of representation therein shall be reduced in the proportion which the number of such male citizens shall bear to the whole number of male citizens twenty-one years of age in such State.

Section 3.

No person shall be a Senator or Representative in Congress, or elector of President and Vice-President, or hold any office, civil or military, under the United States, or under any State, who, having previously taken an oath, as a member of Congress, or as an officer of the United States, or as a member of any State legislature, or as an executive or judicial officer of any State, to support the Constitution of the United States, shall have engaged in insurrection or rebellion against the same, or given aid or comfort to the enemies thereof. But Congress may by a vote of two-thirds of each House, remove such disability.

Section 4.

The validity of the public debt of the United States, authorized by law,

including debts incurred for payment of pensions and bounties for services in suppressing insurrection or rebellion, shall not be questioned. But neither the United States nor any State shall assume or pay any debt or obligation incurred in aid of insurrection or rebellion against the United States, or any claim for the loss or emancipation of any slave; but all such debts, obligations and claims shall be held illegal and void.
Section 5.
The Congress shall have the power to enforce, by appropriate legislation, the provisions of this article.
Changed by section 1 of the 26th amendment.

Amendment XV
Passed by Congress February 26, 1869. Ratified February 3, 1870.
Section 1.
The right of citizens of the United States to vote shall not be denied or abridged by the United States or by any State on account of race, color, or previous condition of servitude--
Section 2.
The Congress shall have the power to enforce this article by appropriate legislation.

Amendment XVI
Passed by Congress July 2, 1909. Ratified February 3, 1913.
Note: Article I, section 9, of the Constitution was modified by amendment 16.
The Congress shall have power to lay and collect taxes on incomes, from whatever source derived, without apportionment among the several States, and without regard to any census or enumeration.

Amendment XVII
Passed by Congress May 13, 1912. Ratified April 8, 1913.
Note: Article I, section 3, of the Constitution was modified by the 17th amendment.
The Senate of the United States shall be composed of two Senators from each State, elected by the people thereof, for six years; and each Senator shall have one vote. The electors in each State shall have the qualifications requisite for electors of the most numerous branch of the State legislatures.
When vacancies happen in the representation of any State in the

Senate, the executive authority of such State shall issue writs of election to fill such vacancies: *Provided,* That the legislature of any State may empower the executive thereof to make temporary appointments until the people fill the vacancies by election as the legislature may direct.

This amendment shall not be so construed as to affect the election or term of any Senator chosen before it becomes valid as part of the Constitution.

Amendment XVIII

Passed by Congress December 18, 1917. Ratified January 16, 1919. Repealed by amendment 21.

Section 1.

After one year from the ratification of this article the manufacture, sale, or transportation of intoxicating liquors within, the importation thereof into, or the exportation thereof from the United States and all territory subject to the jurisdiction thereof for beverage purposes is hereby prohibited.

Section 2.

The Congress and the several States shall have concurrent power to enforce this article by appropriate legislation.

Section 3.

This article shall be inoperative unless it shall have been ratified as an amendment to the Constitution by the legislatures of the several States, as provided in the Constitution, within seven years from the date of the submission hereof to the States by the Congress.

Amendment XIX

Passed by Congress June 4, 1919. Ratified August 18, 1920.

The right of citizens of the United States to vote shall not be denied or abridged by the United States or by any State on account of sex.

Congress shall have power to enforce this article by appropriate legislation.

Amendment XX

Passed by Congress March 2, 1932. Ratified January 23, 1933.

Note: Article I, section 4, of the Constitution was modified by section 2 of this amendment. In addition, a portion of the 12th amendment was superseded by section 3.

Section 1.

The terms of the President and the Vice President shall end at noon on the 20th day of January, and the terms of Senators and Representatives at noon on the 3d day of January, of the years in which such terms would have ended if this article had not been ratified; and the terms of their successors shall then begin.

Section 2.

The Congress shall assemble at least once in every year, and such meeting shall begin at noon on the 3d day of January, unless they shall by law appoint a different day.

Section 3.

If, at the time fixed for the beginning of the term of the President, the President elect shall have died, the Vice President elect shall become President. If a President shall not have been chosen before the time fixed for the beginning of his term, or if the President elect shall have failed to qualify, then the Vice President elect shall act as President until a President shall have qualified; and the Congress may by law provide for the case wherein neither a President elect nor a Vice President shall have qualified, declaring who shall then act as President, or the manner in which one who is to act shall be selected, and such person shall act accordingly until a President or Vice President shall have qualified.

Section 4.

The Congress may by law provide for the case of the death of any of the persons from whom the House of Representatives may choose a President whenever the right of choice shall have devolved upon them, and for the case of the death of any of the persons from whom the Senate may choose a Vice President whenever the right of choice shall have devolved upon them.

Section 5.

Sections 1 and 2 shall take effect on the 15th day of October following the ratification of this article.

Section 6.

This article shall be inoperative unless it shall have been ratified as an amendment to the Constitution by the legislatures of three-fourths of the several States within seven years from the date of its submission.

Amendment XXI

Passed by Congress February 20, 1933. Ratified December 5, 1933.

Section 1.

The eighteenth article of amendment to the Constitution of the United States is hereby repealed.
Section 2.
The transportation or importation into any State, Territory, or Possession of the United States for delivery or use therein of intoxicating liquors, in violation of the laws thereof, is hereby prohibited.
Section 3.
This article shall be inoperative unless it shall have been ratified as an amendment to the Constitution by conventions in the several States, as provided in the Constitution, within seven years from the date of the submission hereof to the States by the Congress.

Amendment XXII

Passed by Congress March 21, 1947. Ratified February 27, 1951.
Section 1.
No person shall be elected to the office of the President more than twice, and no person who has held the office of President, or acted as President, for more than two years of a term to which some other person was elected President shall be elected to the office of President more than once. But this Article shall not apply to any person holding the office of President when this Article was proposed by Congress, and shall not prevent any person who may be holding the office of President, or acting as President, during the term within which this Article becomes operative from holding the office of President or acting as President during the remainder of such term.
Section 2.
This article shall be inoperative unless it shall have been ratified as an amendment to the Constitution by the legislatures of three-fourths of the several States within seven years from the date of its submission to the States by the Congress.

Amendment XXIII

Passed by Congress June 16, 1960. Ratified March 29, 1961.
Section 1.
The District constituting the seat of Government of the United States shall appoint in such manner as Congress may direct:
A number of electors of President and Vice President equal to the whole number of Senators and Representatives in Congress to which the

District would be entitled if it were a State, but in no event more than the least populous State; they shall be in addition to those appointed by the States, but they shall be considered, for the purposes of the election of President and Vice President, to be electors appointed by a State; and they shall meet in the District and perform such duties as provided by the twelfth article of amendment.
Section 2.
The Congress shall have power to enforce this article by appropriate legislation.

Amendment XXIV

Passed by Congress August 27, 1962. Ratified January 23, 1964.
Section 1.
The right of citizens of the United States to vote in any primary or other election for President or Vice President, for electors for President or Vice President, or for Senator or Representative in Congress, shall not be denied or abridged by the United States or any State by reason of failure to pay poll tax or other tax.
Section 2.
The Congress shall have power to enforce this article by appropriate legislation.

Amendment XXV

Passed by Congress July 6, 1965. Ratified February 10, 1967.
Note: Article II, section 1, of the Constitution was affected by the 25th amendment.
Section 1.
In case of the removal of the President from office or of his death or resignation, the Vice President shall become President.
Section 2.
Whenever there is a vacancy in the office of the Vice President, the President shall nominate a Vice President who shall take office upon confirmation by a majority vote of both Houses of Congress.
Section 3.
Whenever the President transmits to the President pro tempore of the Senate and the Speaker of the House of Representatives his written declaration that he is unable to discharge the powers and duties of his office, and until he transmits to them a written declaration to

the contrary, such powers and duties shall be discharged by the Vice President as Acting President.

Section 4.

Whenever the Vice President and a majority of either the principal officers of the executive departments or of such other body as Congress may by law provide, transmit to the President pro tempore of the Senate and the Speaker of the House of Representatives their written declaration that the President is unable to discharge the powers and duties of his office, the Vice President shall immediately assume the powers and duties of the office as Acting President.

Thereafter, when the President transmits to the President pro tempore of the Senate and the Speaker of the House of Representatives his written declaration that no inability exists, he shall resume the powers and duties of his office unless the Vice President and a majority of either the principal officers of the executive department or of such other body as Congress may by law provide, transmit within four days to the President pro tempore of the Senate and the Speaker of the House of Representatives their written declaration that the President is unable to discharge the powers and duties of his office. Thereupon Congress shall decide the issue, assembling within forty-eight hours for that purpose if not in session. If the Congress, within twenty-one days after receipt of the latter written declaration, or, if Congress is not in session, within twenty-one days after Congress is required to assemble, determines by two-thirds vote of both Houses that the President is unable to discharge the powers and duties of his office, the Vice President shall continue to discharge the same as Acting President; otherwise, the President shall resume the powers and duties of his office.

Amendment XXVI

Passed by Congress March 23, 1971. Ratified July 1, 1971.

Note: Amendment 14, section 2, of the Constitution was modified by section 1 of the 26th amendment.

Section 1.

The right of citizens of the United States, who are eighteen years of age or older, to vote shall not be denied or abridged by the United States or by any State on account of age.

Section 2.

The Congress shall have power to enforce this article by appropriate legislation.

Amendment XXVII

Originally proposed Sept. 25, 1789. Ratified May 7, 1992.
No law, varying the compensation for the services of the Senators and Representatives, shall take effect, until an election of representatives shall have intervened.

END

The Bill of Rights and other constitutional amendments are federal regulations that apply to all states. There are also state laws and rights that have been created by the US Congress and Senate. These are far too numerous to mention. An example would include school buses needing to stop before crossing train tracks, and minimum prison sentences required for specific crimes.

> "The freedom and happiness of man...[are] the sole objects of all legitimate government."
> Thomas Jefferson, letter to Thaddeus Kosciusko, 1810

When businesses and government make bad decisions people suffer. All evil in the world can be broken down into bad decisions. The four major causes of bad decisions are immorality, unethical conduct, ignorance and incompetence. The mission of an agnostic is to promote good decisions, which means informed decisions. Good decisions increase the common good. Good decisions will be promoted through morality, the highest ethical conduct, knowledge and competence. One of the major obstacles currently faced in this mission of promoting good decisions is authoritative positions filled by people who are not qualified for the job, but are well connected. Cronyism is a cancer to businesses and the country.

If you took over as CEO of some major corporation, what would your objectives be? Perhaps you would work towards building a positive and ethical corporate culture that's receptive to change. Perhaps you would promote certain changes to the products and services provided by the company. Assuredly, you would take part in major marketing campaigns. You would also analyze metrics that indicates the operating and financial health of the organization. Are you meeting industry standards? Do you have industry quality certifications? What is your market share in various segments in comparison to your competition? How do your products and services compare with competitors? What are your company's strengths and weaknesses? What are your internal costs in marketing, sales, IT, HR, etc. and how do they compare with industry averages?

Once you have information about your company, you are ready to make decisions regarding future direction based upon your vision and how your metrics compares with industry standards and averages. For example, let's suppose you found a corporate cost in a particular segment of your company such as travel expenses that are twice as much as the industry average, or basically what cost your competitors are paying. The logical decision would be to drastically reduce that cost if there is no justification for the high amount. This may require calling a Sr. VP and telling him or her, they have 6 months to reduce the travel cost by a certain percentage.

If you were elected into a high government office the scenario of a CEO would be similar. If you were a town representative you would need metrics on your town such as income, unemployment, tax rate, education, homelessness, crime, etc. in order to properly guide direction and focus. The metrics would indicate what your town needs to improve. If your town has low test scores, education needs to be improved. If your town has high unemployment, the goal and focus needs to be attracting more businesses and jobs.

If you were elected as a state representative your scenario would be similar to a town representative, but you would be analyzing data by your state rather than by your town. Now let's suppose you were elected President of the United States. What would your objectives be? You now have oversight of all 50 states and are also a world leader. The metric that applies to each one of these scenarios is quality of life. Are your workers happy and healthy? Are they motivated? Are the people in your town, state or country living a good life?

In the introduction, I stated this book was about tackling the greatest questions of our existence. How people should live is one of our greatest questions. Freedom and quality of life are directly related to how we should live. How do we raise our quality of life to maximize our health and happiness? Often we don't appreciate what we have till it's gone. Without focusing on what we have and what is important, it's easy to lose our freedoms and quality of life.

> "Any nation that thinks more of its ease and comfort than its freedom will soon lose its freedom; and the ironical thing about it is that it will lose its ease and comfort too."
> – W. Somerset Maugham (1874-1965)

So what is quality of life and how do we measure it? Quality of life is measured physically and psychological. Are we happy and healthy? Opportunity and freedom are directly related to our quality of life. You don't have to be in a high corporate or government position to access information about the living conditions of people across the world that indicates their quality of life.

There are many ways to represent good and bad living conditions among humans. By selecting specific criteria we can then analyze and compare scores from city to city and country to country. For this analysis let's explore just a few of the quality of life popular indicators:

Income Level and GDP
Poverty Level
Infant Mortality Rate
Life Expectancy
Education

> "Government is instituted for the common good; for the protection, safety, prosperity, and happiness of the people; and not for profit, honor, or private interest of any one man, family, or class of men; therefore, the people alone have an incontestable, unalienable, and indefeasible right to institute government; and to reform, alter, or totally change the same, when their protection, safety, prosperity, and happiness require it."
> John Adams, Thoughts on Government, 1776

Income Level and GDP

Gross Domestic Product or GDP refers to the total market value of all goods and services produced by a nation. This includes consumer spending, government spending, and business spending and net exports. The GDP per capita is the gross domestic product of a country divided by its population.

The 10 nations with the highest GDP are currently (www.aneki.com):

Country	Population	GDP Per Capita
Liechtenstein	34,247	$118,000
Qatar	907,229	$101,000
Luxembourg	480,222	$85,100
Kuwait	2,505,559	$60,800
Norway	4,627,926	$57,500
Brunei	374,577	$54,100
Singapore	4,553,009	$52,900
United States	301,139,947	$48,000
Ireland	4,109,086	$47,800
San Marino	29,615	$46,100

The 10 nations with the lowest GDP are currently:

Country	Population	GDP Per Capita
Zimbabwe	12,311,143	$200
Congo, Democratic Republic of the	65,751,512	$300
Burundi	8,390,505	$400
Liberia	3,195,931	$500
Guinea-Bissau	1,472,780	$600
Somalia	9,118,773	$600
Central African Republic	4,369,038	$700
Eritrea	4,906,585	$700
Niger	12,894,865	$700

Sierra Leone	6,144,562	$700

Poverty Level

Through opportunities provided by globalization, 300 million people in China went from below the poverty level to above the poverty level. So what is the poverty level? The World Bank determines the poverty line, and in 2008, this line was $1.25 a day globally. This number has to be adjusted based on each specific nation to account for the wide range of cost of living, and average income levels. Globally, nearly half the world lives on less than $2.50 a day. That represents over three billion people. Approx. 80% of humanity lives on less than $10 a day. (www.globalissues.org)

So what is the poverty line in the United States of America? The following has been obtained by http://aspe.hhs.gov/poverty/09poverty.shtml. As the US is a wealthy nation the poverty level is far above the global poverty line at over $29 a day.

The 2009 Poverty Guidelines for the
48 Contiguous States and the District of Columbia

Persons in family	Poverty guideline
1	$10,830
2	14,570
3	18,310
4	22,050
5	25,790
6	29,530
7	33,270
8	37,010

For families with more than 8 persons, add $3,740 for each additional person.

2009 Poverty Guidelines for
Alaska

Persons in family	Poverty guideline
1	$13,530
2	18,210
3	22,890
4	27,570
5	32,250
6	36,930
7	41,610
8	46,290

For families with more than 8 persons, add $4,680 for each additional person.

2009 Poverty Guidelines for
Hawaii

Persons in family	Poverty guideline
1	$12,460
2	16,760
3	21,060
4	25,360
5	29,660
6	33,960
7	38,260
8	42,560

For families with more than 8 persons, add $4,300 for each additional person.
SOURCE: *Federal Register*, Vol. 74, No. 14, January 23, 2009, pp. 4199–4201

Infant Mortality Rate

Below are the countries with the worst infant mortality rate:

	Country	Infant mortality rate(deaths/1,000 live births)
1	Angola	192.50
2	Afghanistan	165.96
3	Sierra Leone	145.24
4	Mozambique	132.04
5	Liberia	130.51
6	Niger	122.66
7	Somalia	118.52
8	Mali	117.99
9	Tajikistan	112.10
10	Guinea-Bissau	108.72

Below are the countries with the best infant mortality rate:

	Country	Infant mortality rate(deaths/1,000 live births)
1	Singapore	2.28
2	Sweden	2.77
3	Japan	3.28
4	Iceland	3.31
5	Finland	3.59
6	Norway	3.73
7	Malta	3.94
8	Czech Republic	3.97
9	Andorra	4.05
10	Germany	4.20

Life Expectancy

Countries with highest life expectancy:

Rank	Country	Life expectancy at birth (years)	Date of Information
1	Macau	84.36	2009 est.
2	Andorra	82.51	2009 est.
3	Japan	82.12	2009 est.
4	Singapore	81.98	2009 est.
5	San Marino	81.97	2009 est.
6	Hong Kong	81.86	2009 est.
7	Australia	81.63	2009 est.
8	Canada	81.23	2009 est.
9	France	80.98	2009 est.
10	Sweden	80.86	2009 est.

Countries with lowest life expectancy:

Rank	Country	Life expectancy at birth (years)	Date of Information
216	Central African Republic	44.47	2009 est.
217	Malawi	43.82	2009 est.
218	Djibouti	43.37	2009 est.
219	Liberia	41.84	2009 est.
220	Sierra Leone	41.24	2009 est.
221	Mozambique	41.18	2009 est.
222	Lesotho	40.38	2009 est.
223	Zambia	38.63	2009 est.
224	Angola	38.20	2009 est.
225	Swaziland	31.88	2009 est.

Education

Most educated countries include:

	Country	Percentage of population aged 25-64 that have attained a tertiary level of education (OECD Countries)
1	Canada	44.0
2	United States	38.4
3	Japan	37.4
4	Sweden	33.4
5	Finland	33.3
6	Denmark	31.9
7	Australia	31.3
8	Norway	31.0
9	New Zealand	30.9
10	Korea, South	29.5

Countries with highest illiteracy rates include:

Rank	Country	Adult Illiteracy Rate
1	Niger	84.3%
2	Burkina Faso	77.0%
3	Afghanistan	63.7%
4	Sierra Leone	63.7%
5	Gambia, the	63.5%
6	Guinea-Bissau	63.2%
7	Senegal	62.7%
8	Benin	62.5%
9	Ethiopia	61.3%
10	Mauritania	60.1%

Other indicators for quality of life include safety, pollution, access to clean water and food. So what does this all mean? We want a high quality of life for ourselves and our families. We want a high quality of life for our country and other countries. How do we get it?

Let's begin with wealth. Does one need wealth in order to have a healthy body and mind? Much of the world lives in poverty. Can one have a high quality of life when all they have is the piece of dirt they currently happen to be standing or sitting on? A healthy body is virtually impossible with malnutrition and dehydration. For people in poverty medical options are extremely limited for sickness or injury. Quality of life in regard to physical well being is low without some level of assets.

What about psychological quality of life? Can people in poverty be happy? The answer is yes. Money does not buy everything. Instead of being surrounded by computers and televisions, those without means can surround themselves with friends and family. They can surround themselves with people they like and people they love. Often wealth brings unhappiness as it encourages a thirst for instant unquenchable gratification. Many kids today in wealthy nations that have game systems, computers, televisions and iPods are always bored. Buddha taught the way to happiness was to give up all desires, as it was these wants that caused suffering. What do individual suicide rates tell us about happiness in regard to wealth and poverty? The highest individual suicide rates in the world are not in the poorest countries, they are in the wealthiest.

How does a country escape poverty? Means include exploiting natural resources such as oil or precious metals, producing goods such as clothing or food, and providing services such as low cost labor. Attracting tourism is another way to increase GDP per capita. Another way that isn't mentioned often is population control. Often this discussion is avoided as people don't want to play God with other people's lives. We need to get real, and we need to talk about population control.

If the population exceeds the resources the country is able to produce, the natural course is a reduction of the population through starvation. This would be Charles Darwin's natural course of survival of the fittest. By other countries providing "free" food the natural course is altered and the population increases. Is the providing of food charity, or is it cruel if the result is more and more starving people?

- "Give a man a fish and you feed him for a day. Teach him how to fish and you feed him for a lifetime." – Lao Tzu (6th century B.C.)
- "We should measure welfare's success by how many people leave welfare, not by how many are added." – Ronald Reagan (1911-2004)

If providing food is in response to a draught then it is charity. Once the drought is over, the country will be able to produce the food necessary to feed the population. If other countries don't sell food, but give food to another country as a normal habit then it is not charity but cruel. No country wants to be a welfare state. Each country has pride and wants to be independent. The population must be supported by what the country can independently produce or purchase. If it is not, then either the country finds a means to increase food supply, or the population of that country needs to be decreased. Birth control is a controlled humane method of controlling population. Relocation is another means. If one is starving in a desert, then move somewhere else.

> "It is not the strongest of the species that survive, nor the most intelligent, but the one most responsive to change."
> – Charles Darwin (1809-1882)

The quality of life for any people will be extremely low if they have no safety. Currently, in some parts of the world warlords are killing and raping certain groups of people. In order for these people to achieve a better quality of life, they need to be protected. This is one of the responsibilities of the United Nations. The UN was founded in 1945 to promote peace, security and economic development. The United Nations is a powerful entity composed of many strong counties. This entity has the means to do great things, but ultimately needs strong leadership to actually accomplish great things.

Infant mortality is directly tied to wealth. Pregnant women who are malnourished and dehydrated with little or no access to medical resources will have less success in delivery. Life expectancy is related to wealth, but also lifestyle. The life expectancy of Americans and many Europeans may actually decrease due to an epidemic with obesity including child obesity. Do we expect the poorest countries to have the lowest life expectancies? Yes, there is a direct correlation, but it's not one for one. The impact of lifestyle can be provided in the analysis of the US in regard to wealth and life expectancy. By using GDP per capita as the criterion, the United States ranks as the 8th wealthiest country in the world. When it comes to life expectancy; the US rates 50th. Many poorer countries have a higher life expectancy than the US.

What about education? Education is directly tied to the potential of individual people to experience and achieve great things in their life time. Going back to Maslow's hierarchy of needs, the top two levels of the pyramid are:

Self-actualization – Morality, creativity, spontaneity, problem solving, lack of prejudice, acceptance of facts

Esteem – Self-esteem, confidence, achievement, respect of others, respect by others

Education provides the opportunity to live a better life and raise the standard of living. This is the ability to achieve the highest needs in Maslow's hierarchy. This is an opportunity many people do not have. For the people in severe poverty in the world, all time and effort are spent obtaining Maslow's most basic needs. All effort is spent on getting something to eat, clean water, and shelter every single day. They are severely limited in achieving the advanced needs Esteem and Self-actualization.

The greatest gift to the world to raise the standard of living for all people is education.

"You must be the change you wish to see in the world."
– Mahatma Gandhi (1869-1948)

How much is a 40-hour worker entitled to in the US?

"Chose a job you love, and you will never work a day in your life."
— Confucius (551-479B.C.)

I once listened to an atheist promote atheism. He focused on attacking Christianity and making his case that there was no God. When he completed his argument, he went right into promoting communism. I found this very strange. Is the automatic conclusion if one is to be an atheist that they must also be a communist? I just don't see the connection. I'm certainly not an atheist or a communist. I am a capitalist who loves the United States of America. I love my way of life and will fight to keep it.

It's sometimes funny how we are all different, and all individuals. Some things connect with us and some things don't. Religion never connected with me but patriotism did. The more I obtain knowledge and truth the stronger my love for the founding principles of the United States of America becomes. Not surprisingly, as a free thinker, my view of capitalism differs from the norm. I should clarify that my belief in capitalism is a rational one. Capitalism needs structure, regulation and oversight. I'm not a believer that CEOs should receive more money in one month than the average worker makes in a lifetime. This practice leads to arrogance, carelessness, corruption, neglect and incompetence.

In my view of capitalism, I also believe in a safety net for all people; the right to work.

Imagine the world as a large pie that needs to be distributed among the entire population. How big are the pieces? Obviously, some have much larger pieces than others. In America and other wealthy countries, we have large pieces. Here we are sitting around sipping fancy drinks and enjoying all the modern luxuries such as a hot bath any time we want it. Should we feel guilty? I don't believe so. I am by no means a conservationist. I have a nice piece of the pie but do not want my piece smaller so it coincides more evenly with that of the global average. I want the global average piece of the pie to be larger so it coincides better with mine. That is how I view life.

> "In a country well governed poverty is something to be ashamed of. In a country badly governed wealth is something to be ashamed of." — Confucius (551-479B.C.)

For example, let's discuss energy. There are those in the US that want to limit people's use of air conditioning. They want us to use less energy so that we burn less fossil fuel and apparently not require any type of investment to increase energy capacity. As a believer in freedom, I oppose this view. Freedom includes the ability to blast the air conditioning if one can pay the resulting electric bill. Does this mean I don't care about pollution? It absolutely does not. It means I believe in a robust power grid that includes alternative energy and nuclear power. We need to build modern nuclear power plants and work with the world on practical effective ways to discard nuclear waste. Nuclear power does not produce greenhouse gases. I want the pie of electrical power to be enormous so that everyone can have a big piece. I want electricity to be abundant and cheap thereby easily obtainable and easily affordable. We have the people and we have the technology, the only thing stopping us is politics.

It's time to focus on the good old United States of America, and how much 40-hour a week workers should expect to have. What minimum standard of living is a 40-hour worker entitled to? Let's take an example of folks with a good upbringing and a good college education. They have the proper guidance, aptitude and ambition to do well in the working world. Through employment or running their own business, they have a house with a garage, a couple of nice cars, big screen television, retirement accounts, and are able to take their family to Disney World every year. They are doing just fine and have achieved the American dream.

Now let's take an example of people who perhaps didn't have a good upbringing and do not have a college education. Perhaps they don't have high aptitude or ambition. Perhaps they do have high aptitude and ambition, but are lacking opportunity. Either way, they don't currently have high paying employment. These people have what's considered a low skilled job. Do they get the house with a garage, couple of nice cars, big screen television, retirement account and Disney World trips? They do not nor should they in a capitalist society, but what should they have? What should we expect them to have?

An agnostic approach or any method of problem solving is useless if it's not used. In order to solve problems, we need to recognize and focus on the problems. The problems need attention. Some situations require free dialog along with gathering knowledge. There are major issues in any country that must have some focus and be discussed in order to be addressed. The following is my opinion of entitlement in the US. Some of you will agree with me and some of you will not. Everyone should agree that these issues warrant discussion.

Everyone should have the right to employment. This needs to be a top priority, and we absolutely have the ability through the right people and organizations to make this happen. Unemployment is a problem for many countries. In our global economy, we should all work together to find solutions. Solutions may include limiting automation. If everything gets automated, we'll all be out of work. Everybody needs a job. When I visit the downtown area of the great city of Chicago, there are homeless people on the street corners. In winter when it's bitterly cold, they are out there all day long shaking a cup to get money. Anyone who can stand outside all day long in freezing weather shaking a cup is not only capable of work, but of doing a job much easier than what they are currently enduring.

In 1880, a baby girl named Helen Keller was born. A terrible fever left her blind and deaf before her 2nd birthday. An amazing woman by the name of Anne Sullivan taught Helen sign language, which enabled her to communicate from her lonely, dark and silent world with the outside world. In 1904, Helen graduated from Radcliffe College with honors. If Helen Keller can obtain a college degree, there are extremely few excuses for anyone to not have the ability to work.

- "Work banishes those three great evils: boredom, vice and poverty." – Voltaire (1694-1778)
- "True individual freedom cannot exist without economic security and independence. People who are hungry and out of a job are the stuff of which dictatorships are made." Franklin D. Roosevelt (1882-1945)

I am a capitalist. Those who take the opportunities to increase their skills and raise their value in the job market should absolutely be rewarded with the ability to buy more stuff than they were before. At the same time, I believe in a safety net for the poorest of Americans and the folks who need a hand up which includes the right to employment. Would a job program that guarantees employment to anyone seeking it be a cost this country cannot afford? It all depends on people and management. How much does the US spend on unemployment benefits? How much does the US spend on welfare? How much does the US spend on crime and prisons?

People need money to live. If they can't get money through employment, they will find other ways including crime. How much does the US spend for every prisoner in jail? Imagine the impoverished communities in this country. If everyone could at least earn minimum wage, these communities now filled with the unemployed could be revitalized with workers and paychecks. This would stimulate the economies of these neighborhoods and bring in small businesses and more jobs. Through proper management, job programs can be productive and little tax burden to the people. Through proper management, the benefits of the right to work would easily out way the cost of unemployment benefits, welfare, crime and prison sentences that would be reduced as a result.

So let's suppose everyone at least has a right to employment. For the low skilled workers at the bottom of the hourly wage chart working 40 hours per week, what do they get? What is the minimum someone working 40 hours per week should be entitled to? I'm going to break this down in the following categories:

Category	Expectation
Housing	Small Studio
Children	If someone making minimum wage has kids, they may need to work over 40 hours a week possibly including working in a child care program that includes his or her kids in it.
Transportation	Public transportation or a small car. Should be able to work within an hour commute of home.
Education	Should be able to afford 2-6 community college classes per year
Health Care and Dental	Basic programs covering yearly check-ups.
Retirement	Up to 4% of wages per year, 50% match 401k.
Drink	Running water
Food	Grocery store bought food and self preparation. Once a week low to mid restaurant service.
Vacation	Once a year inexpensive vacation
Time Off	At least 2 weeks total sick and vacation time a year and 5 holidays.
Raise	At least a cost of living raise every year
Luxuries	Should be able to afford basic radio, television and computer access. Should be able to afford basic clothing, cooking, furniture, beauty and household items.
Credit	Debit card. Very little or no line of credit.

Once a minimum standard of living for a 40-hour week worker is defined, analysis must be done to identify the challenges of meeting this minimum, and finding solutions to the challenges which will vary from town to town and state to state. Solutions to challenges may include the promotion of low rent apartments, which should not be confused with low income apartments or government housing. Low rent apartments should be accessible to all income levels. By establishing a minimum level of opportunity, we are establishing a minimum level of freedom.

Opportunity and freedom are good. May all people enjoy life, liberty and the pursuit of happiness.

THE DECLARATION OF INDEPENDENCE
AND THE UNITED STATES CONSTITUTION

The Jews have the Old Testament in the Bible. The Catholics and Christians have the Old Testament and New Testament in the Bible. The Muslims have the Qur'an. The Hindus have the ancient Vedas. Taoism has the Tao Te Ching. Every established religion has religious text. So what doctrine exists for agnostics? An agnostic is a free thinker without any boundaries. We can analyze any religion or philosophy for the obtainment of truth. An agnostic initially takes a neutral stance on an argument and analyzes both sides to make an informed decision, or no decision at all if not enough sufficient evidence exists to prove one side over the other, such as the case with religious claims of divinity.

The agnostic has no religious text. The agnostic has all religious text. The agnostic has all religion, philosophy, science, history and every academic and non-academic study and document at his or her disposal. This does pose certain challenges when it comes to promoting agnosticism as a formal system of belief. The documents I hold more sacred than any religious text are the Declaration of Independence and the United States Constitution. These great historical documents were created using an agnostic approach and promote morality and ethics over any religious doctrine.

"We hold these truths to be self-evident, that all men are created equal, that they are endowed by their Creator with certain unalienable Rights, that among these are Life, Liberty and the pursuit of Happiness."

If you believe in this statement, and believe that no harm will be done to good people in a good world in death, then we share the same religion. Unless unworthy through evil acts, all people deserve respect and freedom in who they are, and what they do. They also deserve justice and opportunity. These are natural human rights that are deserved to all people in every part of the world, regardless of country or religion. Devotedly, in my mind, my spirit and my heart, I hold these truths to be self-evident. Some maintain that it's wrong to fight for human rights in other parts of the world as we are then imposing our values on them. These people are wrong. There are universal values and human rights that must be fought for around the world at all times, by all good people.

Many people believe that the human rights dictated in the Declaration of Independence are natural rights, and the will of God. Many others believe these rights come from the greatest moral reason of mankind. Either by God or by man, I hold this spirit of human rights in the highest regard. We must know what is good, promote what is good and defend what is good.

What if the founding fathers of the US didn't use an agnostic approach? Rather than being the first president, George Washington would have been the first king. The United States did not need to change governing structures in order to separate from England; they could have simply created another monarchy. The founding fathers were not required to specify and promote individual rights, why should they? Why would those who are going to rule purposely limit their own power?

The founding fathers created the United States greater and with a higher purpose than themselves. The intent was the greater good, not personal gain. The great US governing doctrine were created by various men of various philosophies, taking the best from history and education to create a powerful country that is for the people. Anyone who believes these documents were formed without heated debate or criticism would be greatly mistaken. The Declaration of Independence and The US Constitution are a result of great open minded thinkers with no boundaries and a common goal.

The following quotes of the greatest founding fathers of the United

States of America, allows us additional insight into who they were, and what they believed in:

1. "Every measure of prudence, therefore, ought to be assumed for the eventual total extirpation of slavery from the United States.... I have, throughout my whole life, held the practice of slavery in... abhorrence."
   John Adams, letter to Evans, June 8, 1819
2. "The Grecians and Romans were strongly possessed of the spirit of liberty but not the principle, for at the time they were determined not to be slaves themselves, they employed their power to enslave the rest of mankind."
   Thomas Paine, The American Crisis, No. 5, March 21, 1778
3. "Our new Constitution is now established, and has an appearance that promises permanency; but in this world nothing can be said to be certain, except death and taxes."
   Benjamin Franklin, letter to Jean-Baptiste Leroy, November 13, 1789
4. "The fabric of American empire ought to rest on the solid basis of THE CONSENT OF THE PEOPLE. The streams of national power ought to flow from that pure, original fountain of all legitimate authority."
   Alexander Hamilton, Federalist No. 22, December 14, 1787
5. "The rights of neutrality will only be respected when they are defended by an adequate power. A nation, despicable by its weakness, forfeits even the privilege of being neutral."
   Alexander Hamilton, Federalist No. 11, 1787
6. "A free people [claim] their rights as derived from the laws of nature, and not as the gift of their chief magistrate."
   Thomas Jefferson, Rights of British America, 1774
7. "But with respect to future debt; would it not be wise and just for that nation to declare in the constitution they are forming that neither the legislature, nor the nation itself can validly contract more debt, than they may pay within their own age, or within the term of 19 years."
   Thomas Jefferson, September 6, 1789

8. "He [King George] has waged cruel war against human nature itself, violating its most sacred right of life and liberty in the persons of a distant people who never offended him, captivating & carrying them into slavery in another hemisphere, or to incur miserable death in their transportation thither."
Thomas Jefferson, deleted portion of a draft of the Declaration of Independence, June, 1776

9. "The greatest good we can do our country is to heal its party divisions and make them one people."
Thomas Jefferson, letter to John Dickinson, July 23, 1801

10. "The most sacred of the duties of a government [is] to do equal and impartial justice to all citizens."
Thomas Jefferson, Note in Destutt de Tracy, 1816

11. "The tree of liberty must be refreshed from time to time with the blood of patriots and tyrants. It is its natural manure."
Thomas Jefferson, letter to William Stephens Smith, November 13, 1787

12. "We must not let our rulers load us with perpetual debt."
Thomas Jefferson, letter to Samuel Kercheval, July 12, 1816

13. "Where the press is free and every man able to read, all is safe."
Thomas Jefferson, letter to Charles Yancey, January 6, 1816

14. "Happily for America, happily, we trust, for the whole human race, they pursued a new and more noble course. They accomplished a revolution which has no parallel in the annals of human society."
James Madison, Federalist No. 14, November 20, 1787

15. "The civil rights of none, shall be abridged on account of religious belief or worship, nor shall any national religion be established, nor shall the full and equal rights of conscience be in any manner, or on any pretext infringed."
James Madison, proposed amendment to the Constitution, given in a speech in the House of Representatives, 1789

16. "Wherever the real power in a Government lies, there is the danger of oppression."
James Madison, letter to Thomas Jefferson, October 17, 1788

17. "A nation under a well regulated government, should permit none to remain uninstructed. It is monarchical and aristocratical government only that requires ignorance for its support."
Thomas Paine, Rights of Man, 1792

18. "I rejoice in a belief that intellectual light will spring up in the dark corners of the earth; that freedom of enquiry will produce liberality of conduct; that mankind will reverse the absurd position that the many were, made for the few; and that they will not continue slaves in one part of the globe, when they can become freemen in another."
George Washington, draft of First Inaugural Address, April 1789

19. "I wish from my soul that the legislature of this State could see a policy of a gradual Abolition of Slavery."
George Washington, letter to Lawrence Lewis, August 4, 1797

20. "If we desire to insult, we must be able to repel it; if we desire to secure peace, one of the most powerful instruments of our rising prosperity, it must be known, that we are at all times ready for War."
George Washington, Annual Message, December 1793

21. "Knowledge is, in every country, the surest basis of public happiness."
George Washington, First Annual Message, January 8, 1790

22. "The foundation of our Empire was not laid in the gloomy age of Ignorance and Superstition, but at an Epoch when the rights of mankind were better understood and more clearly defined, than at any former period"
George Washington, Circular to the States, June 8, 1783

(www.foundingfathers.info)

These historical documents do not belong to any specific religion, race or class. God is mentioned but not specified as belonging to any specific religion. The US Constitution specifies freedom of religion, which was the opposite of the history and the home land the people who wrote it came from. The freedom and individual rights in America promoted freedom and individual rights in the rest of the world. Without freedom of religion, there are no agnostics or other free thinkers.

Are there dark periods in America's history? Absolutely; as there are dark periods in the history of many countries. It is not the founding fathers who are to blame for it is not because of them that dark periods and great injustices in the past occurred, but rather despite them and their teachings. The great ancient Eastern and Western philosophers are dead. The founding fathers of the United States of America are dead. Abraham Lincoln and many other great leaders are dead. They have left their teachings and their wisdom. They have left a road map to a moral and ethical life. It's up to the living to follow this map or foolishly squander the opportunity.

It all began with the Declaration of Independence in 1776. Many people believe the US separation from England was strictly due to taxes. If one actually reads the Declaration, they will find taxes was only part of the equation. Other reasons included free trade, laws and justice. The Declaration states that all men are created equal. Some would argue this only meant white men at the time of writing. I would argue that our founding fathers knew very well what all men meant, and made the ethics of the Declaration at a higher bar then the society at the time could achieve, but future generations could strive for and obtain. To be fair, there is unfortunate racial discrimination in the US Constitution that has since been corrected. Any discrimination based on race or sex is a direct contradiction to the founding philosophy of all people are created equal.

The US Constitution provides a system of government with a balance of power. This is not a democracy, this is a republic. In order to protect minorities they needed to be protected from the tyranny of the majority. Minorities will not gain rights through the majority having a ruling vote in the matter. The US government was constructed to have a balance of power between the legislative, executive and the judicial branch. There is also a division of power between the federal level and the state level.

The US Declaration of Independence and US Constitution are among the greatest documents ever written. The founding fathers have done everything they can to make the US great. The rest is up to the American people. On the great ladder to moral and ethical nirvana, the founding fathers have given America quite a boost. It's now up to Americans to stay where they are, climb the ladder further, or fall.

Ultimately, the US Constitution is only a piece of paper. It is up to the American people to follow it. There are no excuses for failure. If those in Washington are not fighting for the American people, they need to be replaced and higher standards must be set for those who get in. If the USA fails, all Americans are to blame.

Below is the US Declaration of Independence and US Constitution obtained from www.usconstitution.net. The Bill of Rights and Amendments 11-27 are not included in this chapter as they were listed in a previous chapter. If one takes a little time to read these documents, they will be more knowledgeable about the US government than most US citizens.

The Declaration of Independence
In Congress, July 4, 1776
The unanimous Declaration of the thirteen united States of America

When in the Course of human events, it becomes necessary for one people to dissolve the political bands which have connected them with another, and to assume among the powers of the earth, the separate and equal station to which the Laws of Nature and of Nature's God entitle them, a decent respect to the opinions of mankind requires that they should declare the causes which impel them to the separation.

We hold these truths to be self-evident, that all men are created equal, that they are endowed by their Creator with certain unalienable Rights, that among these are Life, Liberty and the pursuit of Happiness. That to secure these rights, Governments are instituted among Men, deriving their just Powers from the consent of the governed, — That whenever any Form of Government becomes destructive of these ends, it is the Right of the People to alter or to abolish it, and to institute new Government, laying its foundation on such principles and organizing its powers in such form, as to them shall seem most likely to effect their Safety and Happiness. Prudence, indeed, will dictate that Governments long established should not be changed for light and transient causes; and accordingly all experience hath shewn, that mankind are more disposed to suffer, while evils are sufferable, than to right themselves by abolishing the forms to which they are accustomed. But when a long train of abuses and usurpations, pursuing invariably the same Object evinces a design to reduce them under absolute Despotism, it is their right, it is their duty, to throw off such Government, and to provide new guards for their future security — Such has been the patient sufferance of these Colonies; and such is now the necessity which constrains them to alter their former Systems of Government. — The history of the present King of Great Britain is a history of repeated injuries and usurpations, all having in direct object the establishment of an absolute Tyranny over these States. To prove this, let facts be submitted to a candid world.

He has refused his Assent to Laws, the most wholesome and necessary for the public good.

He has forbidden his Governors to pass Laws of immediate and pressing importance, unless suspended in their operation till his Assent should be obtained; and when so suspended, he has utterly neglected to attend to them.

He has refused to pass other Laws for the accommodation of large districts of people, unless those people would relinquish the right of Representation in the Legislature, a right inestimable to them and formidable to tyrants only.

He has called together legislative bodies at places unusual, uncomfortable, and distant from the depository of their Public Records, for the sole purpose of fatiguing them into compliance with his measures.

He has dissolved Representative Houses repeatedly, for opposing with manly firmness his invasions on the rights of the people.

He has refused for a long time, after such dissolutions, to cause others to be elected; whereby the Legislative Powers, incapable of Annihilation, have returned to the People at large for their exercise; the State remaining in the mean time exposed to all the dangers of invasion from without, and convulsions within.

He has endeavoured to prevent the population of these States; for that purpose obstructing the Laws for Naturalization of Foreigners; refusing to pass others to encourage their migrations hither, and raising the conditions of new Appropriations of Lands.

He has obstructed the Administration of Justice, by refusing his Assent to Laws for establishing Judiciary Powers.

He has made Judges dependent on his Will alone, for the tenure of their offices, and the amount and payment of their salaries.

He has erected a multitude of New Offices, and sent hither swarms of Officers to harrass our People, and eat out their substance.

He has kept among us, in times of peace, Standing Armies without the Consent of our legislatures.

He has affected to render the Military independent of and superior to the Civil Power.

He has combined with others to subject us to a jurisdiction foreign to our constitution, and unacknowledged by our laws; giving his Assent to their Acts of pretended Legislation:

For Quartering large bodies of armed troops among us:

For protecting them, by a mock Trial, from Punishment for any Murders which they should commit on the Inhabitants of these States:

For cutting off our Trade with all parts of the world:

For imposing Taxes on us without our Consent:

For depriving us in many cases, of the benefits of Trial by Jury:

For transporting us beyond seas to be tried for pretended offences:

For abolishing the free system of English Laws in a neighbouring Province, establishing therein an Arbitrary government, and enlarging its Boundaries so as to render it at once an example and fit instrument for introducing the same absolute rule into these Colonies:

For taking away our Charters, abolishing our most valuable Laws, and altering fundamentally the forms of our Governments:

For suspending our own Legislature, and declaring themselves invested with power to legislate for us in all cases whatsoever.

He has abdicated Government here, by declaring us out of his Protection and waging War against us.

He has plundered our seas, ravaged our Coasts, burnt our towns, and destroyed the lives of our people.

He is at this time transporting large Armies of foreign Mercenaries to compleat the works of death, desolation and tyranny, already begun with circumstances of Cruelty and perfidy scarcely paralleled in the most barbarous ages, and totally unworthy the Head of a civilized nation.

He has constrained our fellow Citizens taken Captive on the high Seas to bear Arms against their Country, to become the executioners of their friends and Brethren, or to fall themselves by their Hands.

He has excited domestic insurrections amongst us, and has endeavoured to bring on the inhabitants of our frontiers, the merciless Indian Savages, whose known rule of warfare, is an undistinguished destruction of all ages, sexes and conditions.

In every stage of these Oppressions we have Petitioned for Redress in the most humble terms: Our repeated Petitions have been answered only by repeated injury. A Prince, whose character is thus marked by every act which may define a Tyrant, is unfit to be the ruler of a free people.

Nor have we been wanting in attention to our Brittish brethren. We have warned them from time to time of attempts by their legislature to extend an unwarrantable jurisdiction over us. We have reminded them of the circumstances of our emigration and settlement here. We have appealed to their native justice and magnanimity, and we have conjured them by the ties of our common kindred to disavow these usurpations, which, would inevitably interrupt our connections and correspondence. They too have been deaf to the voice of justice and of consanguinity. We must, therefore, acquiesce in the necessity, which denounces our Separation, and hold them, as we hold the rest of mankind, Enemies in War, in Peace Friends.

We, therefore, the Representatives of the united States of America, in General Congress, Assembled, appealing to the Supreme Judge of the world for the rectitude of our intentions, do, in the Name, and by Authority of the good People of these Colonies, solemnly publish and declare, That these United Colonies are, and of Right ought to be Free and Independent States; that they are absolved from all Allegiance to the British Crown, and that all political connection between them and the State of Great Britain, is and ought to be totally dissolved; and that as Free and Independent States, they have full Power to levy War, conclude Peace, contract Alliances, establish Commerce, and to do all other Acts and Things which Independent States may of right do.

And for the support of this Declaration, with a firm reliance on the protection of Divine Providence, we mutually pledge to each other our Lives, our Fortunes and our sacred Honor.

The Constitution of the United States
Preamble
We the People of the United States, in Order to form a more perfect

Union, establish Justice, insure domestic Tranquility, provide for the common defence, promote the general Welfare, and secure the Blessings of Liberty to ourselves and our Posterity, do ordain and establish this Constitution for the United States of America.

Article I - The Legislative Branch
Section 1 - The Legislature

All legislative Powers herein granted shall be vested in a Congress of the United States, which shall consist of a Senate and House of Representatives.

Section 2 - The House

The House of Representatives shall be composed of Members chosen every second Year by the People of the several States, and the Electors in each State shall have the Qualifications requisite for Electors of the most numerous Branch of the State Legislature.

No Person shall be a Representative who shall not have attained to the Age of twenty five Years, and been seven Years a Citizen of the United States, and who shall not, when elected, be an Inhabitant of that State in which he shall be chosen.

(Representatives and direct Taxes shall be apportioned among the several States which may be included within this Union, according to their respective Numbers, which shall be determined by adding to the whole Number of free Persons, including those bound to Service for a Term of Years, and excluding Indians not taxed, three fifths of all other Persons.) **(The previous sentence in parentheses was modified by the** 14th Amendment, section 2.) The actual Enumeration shall be made within three Years after the first Meeting of the Congress of the United States, and within every subsequent Term of ten Years, in such Manner as they shall by Law direct. The Number of Representatives shall not exceed one for every thirty Thousand, but each State shall have at Least one Representative; and until such enumeration shall be made, the State of New Hampshire shall be entitled to chuse three, Massachusetts eight, Rhode Island and Providence Plantations one, Connecticut five, New York six, New Jersey four, Pennsylvania eight, Delaware one, Maryland six, Virginia ten, North Carolina five, South Carolina five and Georgia three.

When vacancies happen in the Representation from any State, the

Executive Authority thereof shall issue Writs of Election to fill such Vacancies.

The House of Representatives shall chuse their Speaker and other Officers; and shall have the sole Power of Impeachment.

Section 3 - The Senate

The Senate of the United States shall be composed of two Senators from each State, *(chosen by the Legislature thereof,)* **(The preceding words in parentheses superseded by** 17th Amendment, section 1**.)** for six Years; and each Senator shall have one Vote.

Immediately after they shall be assembled in Consequence of the first Election, they shall be divided as equally as may be into three Classes. The Seats of the Senators of the first Class shall be vacated at the Expiration of the second Year, of the second Class at the Expiration of the fourth Year, and of the third Class at the Expiration of the sixth Year, so that one third may be chosen every second Year; *(and if Vacancies happen by Resignation, or otherwise, during the Recess of the Legislature of any State, the Executive thereof may make temporary Appointments until the next Meeting of the Legislature, which shall then fill such Vacancies.)* **(The preceding words in parentheses were superseded by the** 17th Amendment, section 2**.)**

No person shall be a Senator who shall not have attained to the Age of thirty Years, and been nine Years a Citizen of the United States, and who shall not, when elected, be an Inhabitant of that State for which he shall be chosen.

The Vice President of the United States shall be President of the Senate, but shall have no Vote, unless they be equally divided.

The Senate shall chuse their other Officers, and also a President pro tempore, in the absence of the Vice President, or when he shall exercise the Office of President of the United States.

The Senate shall have the sole Power to try all Impeachments. When sitting for that Purpose, they shall be on Oath or Affirmation. When the President of the United States is tried, the Chief Justice shall preside: And no Person shall be convicted without the Concurrence of two thirds of the Members present.

Judgment in Cases of Impeachment shall not extend further than to removal from Office, and disqualification to hold and enjoy any Office of honor, Trust or Profit under the United States: but the Party convicted shall nevertheless be liable and subject to Indictment, Trial, Judgment and Punishment, according to Law.

Section 4 - Elections, Meetings

The Times, Places and Manner of holding Elections for Senators and Representatives, shall be prescribed in each State by the Legislature thereof; but the Congress may at any time by Law make or alter such Regulations, except as to the Place of Chusing Senators.

The Congress shall assemble at least once in every Year, and such Meeting shall *(be on the first Monday in December,)* **(The preceding words in parentheses were superseded by the** 20th Amendment, section 2.**)** unless they shall by Law appoint a different Day.

Section 5 - Membership, Rules, Journals, Adjournment

Each House shall be the Judge of the Elections, Returns and Qualifications of its own Members, and a Majority of each shall constitute a Quorum to do Business; but a smaller number may adjourn from day to day, and may be authorized to compel the Attendance of absent Members, in such Manner, and under such Penalties as each House may provide.

Each House may determine the Rules of its Proceedings, punish its Members for disorderly Behavior, and, with the Concurrence of two-thirds, expel a Member.

Each House shall keep a Journal of its Proceedings, and from time to time publish the same, excepting such Parts as may in their Judgment require Secrecy; and the Yeas and Nays of the Members of either House on any question shall, at the Desire of one fifth of those Present, be entered on the Journal.

Neither House, during the Session of Congress, shall, without the Consent of the other, adjourn for more than three days, nor to any other Place than that in which the two Houses shall be sitting.

Section 6 - Compensation

(The Senators and Representatives shall receive a Compensation for their Services, to be ascertained by Law, and paid out of the Treasury of the United States.) **(The preceding words in parentheses were modified by the** 27th Amendment.**)** They shall in all Cases, except Treason, Felony and Breach of the Peace, be privileged from Arrest during their Attendance at the Session of their respective Houses, and in going to

and returning from the same; and for any Speech or Debate in either House, they shall not be questioned in any other Place.

No Senator or Representative shall, during the Time for which he was elected, be appointed to any civil Office under the Authority of the United States which shall have been created, or the Emoluments whereof shall have been increased during such time; and no Person holding any Office under the United States, shall be a Member of either House during his Continuance in Office.

Section 7 - Revenue Bills, Legislative Process, Presidential Veto

All bills for raising Revenue shall originate in the House of Representatives; but the Senate may propose or concur with Amendments as on other Bills.

Every Bill which shall have passed the House of Representatives and the Senate, shall, before it become a Law, be presented to the President of the United States; If he approve he shall sign it, but if not he shall return it, with his Objections to that House in which it shall have originated, who shall enter the Objections at large on their Journal, and proceed to reconsider it. If after such Reconsideration two thirds of that House shall agree to pass the Bill, it shall be sent, together with the Objections, to the other House, by which it shall likewise be reconsidered, and if approved by two thirds of that House, it shall become a Law. But in all such Cases the Votes of both Houses shall be determined by Yeas and Nays, and the Names of the Persons voting for and against the Bill shall be entered on the Journal of each House respectively. If any Bill shall not be returned by the President within ten Days (Sundays excepted) after it shall have been presented to him, the Same shall be a Law, in like Manner as if he had signed it, unless the Congress by their Adjournment prevent its Return, in which Case it shall not be a Law.

Every Order, Resolution, or Vote to which the Concurrence of the Senate and House of Representatives may be necessary (except on a question of Adjournment) shall be presented to the President of the United States; and before the Same shall take Effect, shall be approved by him, or being disapproved by him, shall be repassed by two thirds of the Senate and House of Representatives, according to the Rules and Limitations prescribed in the Case of a Bill.

Section 8 - Powers of Congress

The Congress shall have Power To lay and collect Taxes, Duties, Imposts and Excises, to pay the Debts and provide for the common Defence and general Welfare of the United States; but all Duties, Imposts and Excises shall be uniform throughout the United States;

To borrow money on the credit of the United States;

To regulate Commerce with foreign Nations, and among the several States, and with the Indian Tribes;

To establish an uniform Rule of Naturalization, and uniform Laws on the subject of Bankruptcies throughout the United States;

To coin Money, regulate the Value thereof, and of foreign Coin, and fix the Standard of Weights and Measures;

To provide for the Punishment of counterfeiting the Securities and current Coin of the United States;

To establish Post Offices and Post Roads;

To promote the Progress of Science and useful Arts, by securing for limited Times to Authors and Inventors the exclusive Right to their respective Writings and Discoveries;

To constitute Tribunals inferior to the supreme Court;

To define and punish Piracies and Felonies committed on the high Seas, and Offenses against the Law of Nations;

To declare War, grant Letters of Marque and Reprisal, and make Rules concerning Captures on Land and Water;

To raise and support Armies, but no Appropriation of Money to that Use shall be for a longer Term than two Years;

To provide and maintain a Navy;

To make Rules for the Government and Regulation of the land and naval Forces;

To provide for calling forth the Militia to execute the Laws of the Union, suppress Insurrections and repel Invasions;

To provide for organizing, arming, and disciplining the Militia, and for governing such Part of them as may be employed in the Service of the United States, reserving to the States respectively, the Appointment of the Officers, and the Authority of training the Militia according to the discipline prescribed by Congress;

To exercise exclusive Legislation in all Cases whatsoever, over such District (not exceeding ten Miles square) as may, by Cession of particular States, and the acceptance of Congress, become the Seat of the Government of the United States, and to exercise like Authority over all Places purchased by the Consent of the Legislature of the State in which the Same shall be, for the Erection of Forts, Magazines, Arsenals, dock-Yards, and other needful Buildings; And

To make all Laws which shall be necessary and proper for carrying into Execution the foregoing Powers, and all other Powers vested by this Constitution in the Government of the United States, or in any Department or Officer thereof.

Section 9 - Limits on Congress

The Migration or Importation of such Persons as any of the States now existing shall think proper to admit, shall not be prohibited by the Congress prior to the Year one thousand eight hundred and eight, but a tax or duty may be imposed on such Importation, not exceeding ten dollars for each Person.

The privilege of the Writ of Habeas Corpus shall not be suspended, unless when in Cases of Rebellion or Invasion the public Safety may require it.

No Bill of Attainder or ex post facto Law shall be passed.

(No capitation, or other direct, Tax shall be laid, unless in Proportion to the Census or Enumeration herein before directed to be taken.) **(Section in parentheses clarified by the** 16th Amendment.**)**

No Tax or Duty shall be laid on Articles exported from any State.

No Preference shall be given by any Regulation of Commerce or Revenue to the Ports of one State over those of another: nor shall Vessels bound to, or from, one State, be obliged to enter, clear, or pay Duties in another.

No Money shall be drawn from the Treasury, but in Consequence of Appropriations made by Law; and a regular Statement and Account of the Receipts and Expenditures of all public Money shall be published from time to time.

No Title of Nobility shall be granted by the United States: And no Person holding any Office of Profit or Trust under them, shall, without the Consent of the Congress, accept of any present, Emolument, Office, or Title, of any kind whatever, from any King, Prince or foreign State.

Section 10 - Powers prohibited of States

No State shall enter into any Treaty, Alliance, or Confederation; grant Letters of Marque and Reprisal; coin Money; emit Bills of Credit; make any Thing but gold and silver Coin a Tender in Payment of Debts; pass any Bill of Attainder, ex post facto Law, or Law impairing the Obligation of Contracts, or grant any Title of Nobility.

No State shall, without the Consent of the Congress, lay any Imposts or Duties on Imports or Exports, except what may be absolutely necessary for executing it's inspection Laws: and the net Produce of all Duties and Imposts, laid by any State on Imports or Exports, shall be for the Use of the Treasury of the United States; and all such Laws shall be subject to the Revision and Controul of the Congress.

No State shall, without the Consent of Congress, lay any duty of Tonnage, keep Troops, or Ships of War in time of Peace, enter into any Agreement or Compact with another State, or with a foreign Power, or engage in War, unless actually invaded, or in such imminent Danger as will not admit of delay.

Article II - The Executive Branch
Section 1 - The President

The executive Power shall be vested in a President of the United States of America. He shall hold his Office during the Term of four Years, and, together with the Vice-President chosen for the same Term, be elected, as follows:

Each State shall appoint, in such Manner as the Legislature thereof may direct, a Number of Electors, equal to the whole Number of Senators and Representatives to which the State may be entitled in the Congress: but no Senator or Representative, or Person holding an Office of Trust or Profit under the United States, shall be appointed an Elector.

(The Electors shall meet in their respective States, and vote by Ballot for two persons, of whom one at least shall not lie an Inhabitant of the same State with themselves. And they shall make a List of all the Persons voted for, and of the Number of Votes for each; which List they shall sign and certify, and transmit sealed to the Seat of the Government of the United States, directed to the President of the Senate. The President of the Senate shall, in the Presence of the Senate and House of Representatives, open all the Certificates, and the Votes shall then be counted. The Person having

the greatest Number of Votes shall be the President, if such Number be a Majority of the whole Number of Electors appointed; and if there be more than one who have such Majority, and have an equal Number of Votes, then the House of Representatives shall immediately chuse *by Ballot one of them for President; and if no Person have a Majority, then from the five highest on the List the said House shall in like Manner* chuse *the President. But in* chusing *the President, the Votes shall be taken by States, the Representation from each State having one Vote; a* quorum *for this Purpose shall consist of a Member or Members from two-thirds of the States, and a Majority of all the States shall be necessary to a Choice. In every Case, after the Choice of the President, the Person having the greatest Number of Votes of the Electors shall be the Vice President. But if there should remain two or more who have equal Votes, the Senate shall* chuse *from them by Ballot the Vice-President.)* **(This clause in parentheses was superseded by the** 12th **Amendment.)**

The Congress may determine the Time of chusing the Electors, and the Day on which they shall give their Votes; which Day shall be the same throughout the United States.

No person except a natural born Citizen, or a Citizen of the United States, at the time of the Adoption of this Constitution, shall be eligible to the Office of President; neither shall any Person be eligible to that Office who shall not have attained to the Age of thirty-five Years, and been fourteen Years a Resident within the United States.

(In Case of the Removal of the President from Office, or of his Death, Resignation, or Inability to discharge the Powers and Duties of the said Office, the same shall devolve on the Vice President, and the Congress may by Law provide for the Case of Removal, Death, Resignation or Inability, both of the President and Vice President, declaring what Officer shall then act as President, and such Officer shall act accordingly, until the Disability be removed, or a President shall be elected.) **(This clause in parentheses has been modified by the** 20th **and** 25th **Amendments.)**

The President shall, at stated Times, receive for his Services, a Compensation, which shall neither be increased nor diminished during the Period for which he shall have been elected, and he shall not receive within that Period any other Emolument from the United States, or any of them.

Before he enter on the Execution of his Office, he shall take the following Oath or Affirmation:

"I do solemnly swear (or affirm) that I will faithfully execute the Office of President of the United States, and will to the best of my Ability, preserve, protect and defend the Constitution of the United States."

Section 2 - Civilian Power over Military, Cabinet, Pardon Power, Appointments

The President shall be Commander in Chief of the Army and Navy of the United States, and of the Militia of the several States, when called into the actual Service of the United States; he may require the Opinion, in writing, of the principal Officer in each of the executive Departments, upon any subject relating to the Duties of their respective Offices, and he shall have Power to Grant Reprieves and Pardons for Offenses against the United States, except in Cases of Impeachment.

He shall have Power, by and with the Advice and Consent of the Senate, to make Treaties, provided two thirds of the Senators present concur; and he shall nominate, and by and with the Advice and Consent of the Senate, shall appoint Ambassadors, other public Ministers and Consuls, Judges of the supreme Court, and all other Officers of the United States, whose Appointments are not herein otherwise provided for, and which shall be established by Law: but the Congress may by Law vest the Appointment of such inferior Officers, as they think proper, in the President alone, in the Courts of Law, or in the Heads of Departments.

The President shall have Power to fill up all Vacancies that may happen during the Recess of the Senate, by granting Commissions which shall expire at the End of their next Session.

Section 3 - State of the Union, Convening Congress

He shall from time to time give to the Congress Information of the State of the Union, and recommend to their Consideration such Measures as he shall judge necessary and expedient; he may, on extraordinary Occasions, convene both Houses, or either of them, and in Case of Disagreement between them, with Respect to the Time of Adjournment, he may adjourn them to such Time as he shall think proper; he shall receive Ambassadors and other public Ministers; he shall take Care that the Laws be faithfully executed, and shall Commission all the Officers of the United States.

Section 4 - Disqualification

The President, Vice President and all civil Officers of the United States, shall be removed from Office on Impeachment for, and Conviction of, Treason, Bribery, or other high Crimes and Misdemeanors.

Article III - The Judicial Branch
Section 1 - Judicial powers

The judicial Power of the United States, shall be vested in one supreme Court, and in such inferior Courts as the Congress may from time to time ordain and establish. The Judges, both of the supreme and inferior Courts, shall hold their Offices during good Behavior, and shall, at stated Times, receive for their Services a Compensation which shall not be diminished during their Continuance in Office.

Section 2 - Trial by Jury, Original Jurisdiction, Jury Trials

(The judicial Power shall extend to all Cases, in Law and Equity, arising under this Constitution, the Laws of the United States, and Treaties made, or which shall be made, under their Authority; to all Cases affecting Ambassadors, other public Ministers and Consuls; to all Cases of admiralty and maritime Jurisdiction*; to Controversies to which the United States shall be a Party; to Controversies between two or more States; between a State and Citizens of another State; between Citizens of different States; between Citizens of the same State claiming Lands under Grants of different States, and between a State, or the Citizens thereof, and foreign States, Citizens or Subjects.)* **(This section in parentheses is modified by the 11th Amendment.)**

In all Cases affecting Ambassadors, other public Ministers and Consuls, and those in which a State shall be Party, the supreme Court shall have original Jurisdiction. In all the other Cases before mentioned, the supreme Court shall have appellate Jurisdiction, both as to Law and Fact, with such Exceptions, and under such Regulations as the Congress shall make.

The Trial of all Crimes, except in Cases of Impeachment, shall be by Jury; and such Trial shall be held in the State where the said Crimes shall have been committed; but when not committed within any State, the Trial shall be at such Place or Places as the Congress may by Law have directed.

Section 3 - Treason

Treason against the United States, shall consist only in levying War against them, or in adhering to their Enemies, giving them Aid and Comfort. No Person shall be convicted of Treason unless on the Testimony of two Witnesses to the same overt Act, or on Confession in open Court.

The Congress shall have power to declare the Punishment of Treason, but no Attainder of Treason shall work Corruption of Blood, or Forfeiture except during the Life of the Person attainted.

Article IV - The States
Section 1 - Each State to Honor all others

Full Faith and Credit shall be given in each State to the public Acts, Records, and judicial Proceedings of every other State. And the Congress may by general Laws prescribe the Manner in which such Acts, Records and Proceedings shall be proved, and the Effect thereof.

Section 2 - State citizens, Extradition

The Citizens of each State shall be entitled to all Privileges and Immunities of Citizens in the several States.

A Person charged in any State with Treason, Felony, or other Crime, who shall flee from Justice, and be found in another State, shall on demand of the executive Authority of the State from which he fled, be delivered up, to be removed to the State having Jurisdiction of the Crime.

(No Person held to Service or Labour in one State, under the Laws thereof, escaping into another, shall, in Consequence of any Law or Regulation therein, be discharged from such Service or Labour, But shall be delivered up on Claim of the Party to whom such Service or Labour may be due.)
(This clause in parentheses is superseded by the 13th Amendment.)

Section 3 - New States

New States may be admitted by the Congress into this Union; but no new States shall be formed or erected within the Jurisdiction of any other State; nor any State be formed by the Junction of two or more

States, or parts of States, without the Consent of the Legislatures of the States concerned as well as of the Congress.

The Congress shall have Power to dispose of and make all needful Rules and Regulations respecting the Territory or other Property belonging to the United States; and nothing in this Constitution shall be so construed as to Prejudice any Claims of the United States, or of any particular State.

Section 4 - Republican government

The United States shall guarantee to every State in this Union a Republican Form of Government, and shall protect each of them against Invasion; and on Application of the Legislature, or of the Executive (when the Legislature cannot be convened) against domestic Violence.

Article V - Amendment

The Congress, whenever two thirds of both Houses shall deem it necessary, shall propose Amendments to this Constitution, or, on the Application of the Legislatures of two thirds of the several States, shall call a Convention for proposing Amendments, which, in either Case, shall be valid to all Intents and Purposes, as part of this Constitution, when ratified by the Legislatures of three fourths of the several States, or by Conventions in three fourths thereof, as the one or the other Mode of Ratification may be proposed by the Congress; Provided that no Amendment which may be made prior to the Year One thousand eight hundred and eight shall in any Manner affect the first and fourth Clauses in the Ninth Section of the first Article; and that no State, without its Consent, shall be deprived of its equal Suffrage in the Senate.

Article VI - Debts, Supremacy, Oaths

All Debts contracted and Engagements entered into, before the Adoption of this Constitution, shall be as valid against the United States under this Constitution, as under the Confederation.

This Constitution, and the Laws of the United States which shall be made in Pursuance thereof; and all Treaties made, or which shall be made, under the Authority of the United States, shall be the supreme Law of the Land; and the Judges in every State shall be bound thereby, any Thing in the Constitution or Laws of any State to the Contrary notwithstanding.

The Senators and Representatives before mentioned, and the Members of the several State Legislatures, and all executive and judicial Officers, both of the United States and of the several States, shall be bound by Oath or Affirmation, to support this Constitution; but no religious Test shall ever be required as a Qualification to any Office or public Trust under the United States.

Article VII - Ratification Documents

The Ratification of the Conventions of nine States, shall be sufficient for the Establishment of this Constitution between the States so ratifying the Same.

TIMELESS WISDOM IN
VARIOUS BITS AND PIECES AND SOURCES

When studying great philosophers such as Confucius and Socrates one can find wisdom that transcends the age in which it was written. Much wisdom written thousands of years ago is still true today and always will be from the beginning of mankind to the end.

I have taken quotes from various sources through an agnostic point of view. The great advantage to the agnostic approach is the vastness of which one can obtain knowledge. An agnostic is not limited to specific authors, countries, religions or people. Wisdom is found mostly in the dead. Wisdom can be found in friends and enemies, and in all places. The world is an open oyster. The quotes and proverbs I list are not biased towards any religious belief, or specific group of people. I selected quotes and proverbs that apply to everyone and are timeless with admittedly my own partiality. Of the hundreds of thousands of quotes available, no individual would have the same selection of "the best" as another. I have numbered the quotes and proverbs as reference. They are in no particular order. As too much wisdom may cause the brain to explode, I also included some humor.

1. "I think, therefore I am." -- René Descartes (1596-1650)
2. "I am what I am." – Popeye the Sailor (1929-?)
3. "The unexamined life is not worth living." -- Socrates (quoted by Plato in Apology)

4. "I can't complain but sometimes I still do life's been good to me so far" – Joe Walsh
5. "If you can't be with the one you love, honey, love the one you're with." – Stephen Stills
6. "Let anyone among you who is without sin be the first to throw a stone" – Jesus Christ
7. "Let us be worthy of those who pin their hopes on us." – Yasser Arafat (1929-2004)
8. "It is not worthy of a speaker of truth to curse people." – Prophet Muhammad (570-632)
9. "Nature has given us two ears, two eyes, and but one tongue-to the end that we should hear and see more than we speak." – Socrates (469-399 B.C.)
10. "Before you criticize a man, walk a mile in his shoes. That way, when you do criticize him, you'll be a mile away and have his shoes." – Unknown Source
11. "Happiness is when what you think, what you say, and what you do are in harmony." – Mahatma Gandhi (1869-1948)
12. "Know thyself" – Socrates (469-399 B.C.)
13. "Once the game is over, the king and the pawn go back into the same box." – Italian Proverb
14. "The beginning of wisdom is a definition of terms." – Socrates (469-399 B.C.)
15. "We can easily forgive a child who is afraid of the dark; the real tragedy of life is when men are afraid of the light." – Plato (427-347 B.C.)
16. "Knowledge becomes evil if the aim be not virtuous." – Plato (427-347 B.C.)
17. "It's not that I'm so smart, it's just that I stay with problems longer." – Albert Einstein (1879-1955)
18. "When men speak ill of thee, live so as nobody may believe them." – Plato (427-347 B.C.)
19. "We are twice armed if we fight with faith." – Plato (427-347 B.C.)
20. "The excessive increase of anything causes a reaction in the opposite direction." – Plato (427-347 B.C.)

21. "I have just three things to teach: simplicity, patience, compassion. These three are your greatest treasures." – Lao Tzu (6th century B.C.)

22. "Rhetoric is the art of ruling the minds of men." – Plato (427-347 B.C.)

23. "Wise men talk because they have something to say; fools, because they have to say something." – Plato (427-347 B.C.)

24. "The punishment which the wise suffer who refuse to take part in the government, is to live under the government of worse men." – Plato (427-347 B.C.)

25. "The ideal man bears the accidents of life with dignity and grace, making the best of circumstances." – Aristotle (384-322 B.C.)

26. "The foundation stones for a balanced success are honesty, character, integrity, faith, love and loyalty." – Zig Ziglar

27. "The roots of education are bitter, but the fruit is sweet." – Aristotle (384-322 B.C.)

28. "No great genius has ever existed without some touch of madness." – Aristotle (384-322 B.C.)

29. "It was through the feeling of wonder that men now and at first began to philosophize." – Aristotle (384-322 B.C.)

30. "We are what we repeatedly do. Excellence, then, is not an act, but a habit." – Aristotle (384-322 B.C.)

31. "If you treat your wife like a thoroughbred, you'll never end up with a nag." – Zig Ziglar

32. "The harder you work, the harder it is to surrender." – Vince Lombardi (1913-1970)

33. "Character is that which reveals moral purpose, exposing the class of things a man chooses or avoids." – Aristotle (384-322 B.C.)

34. "The worst form of inequality is to try to make unequal things equal." – Aristotle (384-322 B.C.)

35. "Some have been thought brave because they didn't have the courage to run away." – Proverb

36. "When planning for a year, plant corn. When planning for a decade, plant trees. When planning for life, train and educate people." – Chinese Proverb

37. "No bees, no honey; no work, no money." -- Proverb
38. "Hope for the best, but prepare for the worst." – English Proverb
39. "The greatest conqueror is he who overcomes the enemy without a blow." – Chinese Proverb
40. "A smooth sea never made a skillful mariner." – English Proverb
41. "Practice what you preach." – English Proverb
42. "Take the world as it is, not as it ought to be." – German Proverb
43. "I felt sorry for myself because I had no shoes, until I met a man who had no feet." – Jewish Proverb
44. "Kind words are worth much and they cost little." – Proverb
45. "The wise person has long ears and a short tongue." – German Proverb
46. "Among the blind the one eyed is king." – Proverb
47. "Many a true word is spoken in jest." – English Proverb
48. "Kindness begets kindness." – Greek Proverb
49. "Beliefs have the power to create and the power to destroy. Human beings have the awesome ability to take any experience of their lives and create a meaning that disempowers them or one that can literally save their lives." – Tony Robbins
50. "Better to ask a question than to remain ignorant." – Proverb
51. "Simplicity is the seal of truth." – Proverb
52. "The just man may sin with an open chest of gold before him." – Italian Proverb
53. "At a round table there is no dispute about place." – Italian Proverb
54. "Cunning surpasses strength." – German Proverb
55. "Those who do not study are only cattle dressed up in men's clothes." – Chinese Proverb
56. "Milk the cow, but do not pull off the udder." – Greek Proverb
57. "Persuasion is better than force." – Proverb
58. "Where there's a will, there's a way." – English Proverb
59. "Necessity unites." – German Proverb
60. "Rebuke with soft words and hard arguments." – Proverb

61. "Every cloud has a silver lining." – Proverb
62. "One can easily judge the character of a person by the way they treat people who can do nothing for them." – Proverb
63. "Some people are born hammers, others anvils." – Proverb
64. "Charity sees the need, not the cause." – German Proverb
65. "Examine what is said, not him who speaks." – Arabian Proverb
66. "No one is as angry as the person who is wrong." – Proverb
67. "A little man often casts a long shadow." – Italian Proverb
68. "A stumble may prevent a fall." – English Proverb
69. "As you make your bed, so you must lie in it." – English Proverb
70. "Grey hair is a sign of age, not of wisdom." – Greek Proverb
71. "The time to make friends is before you need them." – Proverb
72. "He who asks is a fool for five minutes, but he who does not ask remains a fool forever." – Chinese Proverb
73. "If a man fools me once, shame on him. If he fools me twice, shame on me." – Chinese Proverb
74. "A fool and his money are soon parted." – Proverb
75. "The fire you kindle for your enemy often burns yourself more than him." – Chinese Proverb
76. "Six feet of Earth make all men equal." – Proverb
77. "By bravely enduring it, an evil which cannot be avoided is overcome." – Proverb
78. "No answer is also an answer." – German Proverb
79. "Well, there's a remedy for all things but death, which will be sure to lay us flat one time or other." – Miguel de Cervantes (1547-1616)
80. "Twenty years from now you will be more disappointed by the things that you didn't do that by the ones you did do. So throw off the bowlines. Sail away from the safe harbor. Catch the trade winds in your sails. Explore. Dream. Discover. – Mark Twain (1835-1910)
81. "The superior man is modest in his speech but exceeds in his actions." – Confucius (551-479B.C.)

82. "What you are will show in what you do." Thomas Edison (1847-1931)

83. "Words may show a man's wit but actions his meaning." – Benjamin Franklin (1706-1790)

84. "Whatever you do may seem insignificant, but it is most important that you do it." – Mahatma Gandhi (1869-1948)

85. "Knowing is not enough; we must apply. Willing is not enough; we must do." – Johann Wolfgang Von Goethe (1749-1832)

86. "Get action. Seize the moment. Man was never intended to become an oyster." – Theodore Roosevelt (1858-1919)

87. "Act as if what you do makes a difference. It does." – William James (1842-1910)

88. "It's no good agreeing with a person who can't make up his mind." – Unknown Source

89. "If your sword's too short, add to its length by taking one step forward." – Unknown Source

90. "Judge each day not by the harvest you reap but by the seeds you plant." – Robert Louis Stevenson (1850-1895)

91. "The ultimate measure of a man is not where he stands in moments of comfort and convenience, but where he stands at times of challenge and controversy." – Martin Luther King Jr. (1929-1968)

92. "Two frogs fell into a bowl of cream. One didn't panic, he relaxed and drowned. The other kicked and struggled so much that the cream turned into butter and he walked out." – Unknown Source

93. "What doesn't kill us makes us stronger." – Friedrich Nietzsche (1844-1900)

94. "In times of storm, the shallowness of the root structure is revealed." – Unknown Source

95. "We see many who are struggling against adversity who are happy, and more although abounding in wealth, who are wretched." – Publius Cornelius Tacitus (55-117)

96. "The world breaks everyone and afterward many are stronger at the broken places." – Ernest Hemmingway (1898-1961)

97. "Adversity is the first path to truth." – Lord Byron (1788-1824)

98. "Every man is the creature of the age in which he lives; very few are able to raise themselves above the ideas of the time." – Voltaire (1694-1778)

99. "With mirth and laughter let old wrinkles come." – William Shakespeare (1564-1616)

100. "Age imprints more wrinkles in the mind than it does on the face." – Michel Eyquem de Montaigne (1533-1592)

101. "Methuselah lived to be 969 years old. You boys and girls will see more in the next fifty years then Methuselah saw in his whole lifetime." – Mark Twain (1835-1910)

102. "The quality, not the longevity, of one's life is what is important." – Martin Luther King Jr. (1929-1968)

103. "If art is to nourish the roots of our culture, society must set the artist free to follow his vision wherever it takes him." – John F. Kennedy (1917-1963)

104. "An army of sheep led by a lion would defeat an army of lions led by a sheep." – Arab Proverb

105. "You can't expect to meet the challenges of today with yesterday's tools and expect to be in business tomorrow." – Unknown Source

106. "Progress is impossible without change, and those who cannot change their minds cannot change anything." – George Bernard Shaw (1856 – 1950)

107. "In order to change, we must be sick and tired or being sick and tired." – Unknown Source

108. "Men of genius are admired, men of wealth are envied, men of power are feared; but only men of character are trusted." – Unknown Source

109. "The measure of a man's real character is what he would do if he knew he would never be found out." – Thomas B. Macaulay (1800-1859)

110. "Clear conscience never fears midnight knocking." – Chinese Proverb

111. "We should be too big to take offense and too noble to give it." – Abraham Lincoln (1809-1865)

112. "Dignity does not consist in possessing honors, but in deserving them." – Aristotle (384-322B.C.)

113. "Courage is resistance to fear, mastery of fear – not absence of fear." – Mark Twain (1835-1910)
114. "We can never be certain of our courage until we have faced danger." – Francois de La Rochefoucauld (1613-1680)
115. "It is curious that physical courage should be so common in the world, and moral courage so rare." – Mark Twain (1835-1910)
116. "We must build dikes of courage to hold back the flood of fear." – Martin Luther King Jr. (1929-1968)
117. "Courage is rightly considered the foremost of the virtues, for upon it, all others depend." – Winston Churchill (1874-1965)
118. "When a resolute young fellow steps up to the great bully, the world, and takes him boldly by the beard, he is often surprised to find it comes off in his hand, and that it was only tied on to scare away the timid adventurers." – Ralph Waldo Emerson (1803-1882)
119. "He who opens a school door, closes a prison." Victor Hugo (1802-1885)
120. "If a man empties his purse into his head, no man can take it away from him. An investment in knowledge always pays the best interest." – Benjamin Franklin (1706-1790)
121. "Those who trust us educate us." – George Eliot (1819-1880)
122. "There is no education like adversity." Benjamin Disraeli (1804-1881)
123. "Education is the progressive realization of our ignorance." Albert Einstein (1879-1955)
124. "An education isn't how much you have committed to memory, or even how much you know. It's being able to differentiate between what you do know and what you don't." Anatole France (1844-1924)
125. "To educate a man in mind and not in morals is to educate a menace to society." – Theodore Roosevelt (1858-1919)
126. "An educational system isn't worth a great deal if it teaches young people how to make a living but doesn't teach them how to make a life." – Unknown Source

127. "On the education of the people of this country the fate of the country depends." – Benjamin Disraeli (1804-1881)
128. "The only thing to fear is fear itself." – Franklin D. Roosevelt (1882-1945)
129. "Let us never negotiate out of fear but let us never fear to negotiate." – John F. Kennedy (1917-1963)
130. "Inaction breeds doubt and fear. Action breeds confidence and courage. If you want to conquer fear, do not sit home and think about it. Go out and get busy." – Dale Carnegie (1888-1955)
131. "Men fear death as children fear to go in the dark; and as that natural fear in children is increased with tales, so is the other." – Francis Bacon (1561-1626)
132. "In the long history of the world, only a few generations have been granted the role of defending freedom in its hour of maximum danger. I do not shrink from this responsibility – I welcome it." – John F. Kennedy (1917-1963)
133. "Some cause happiness wherever they go; others whenever they go." – Oscar Wilde (1854-1900)
134. "Everyone is entitled to my opinion." -- Madonna
135. "The two enemies of human happiness are pain and boredom." – Arthur Schopenhauer (1788-1860)
136. "If you have knowledge, let others light their candles with it." – Winston Churchill (1874-1965)
137. "My philosophy is that not only are you responsible for your life, but doing the best at this moment puts you in the best place for the next moment." – Oprah Winfrey
138. "I am not young enough to know everything." – Oscar Wilde (1854-1900)
139. "I think education is power. I think that being able to communicate with people is power. One of my main goals on this planet is to encourage people to empower themselves." – Oprah Winfrey
140. "Knowledge is power." – Francis Bacon (1561-1626)
141. "When men are pure, laws are useless; when men are corrupt, laws are broken." – Benjamin Disraeli (1804-1881)

142. "Certainly one of the highest duties of the citizen is a scrupulous obedience to the laws of the nation. But it is not the highest duty." – Thomas Jefferson (1743-1826)

143. "Law and order exist for the purpose of establishing justice and when they fail in this purpose they become the dangerously structured dams that block the flow of social progress." – Martin Luther King Jr. (1929-1968)

144. "A jury too often has at least one member more ready to hang the panel than to hang the traitor." – Abraham Lincoln (1809-1865)

145. "Possession is nine tenths of the law." – Proverb

146. "And in the end, it's not the years in your life that count. It's the life in your years." – Abraham Lincoln (1809-1865)

147. "In three words I can sum up everything I've learned about life. It goes on." – Robert Frost (1875-1963)

148. "I don't want to get to the end of my life and find that I have just lived the length of it. I want to have lived the width of it as well." – Diane Ackerman

149. "Life is short and we have never too much time for gladdening the hearts of those who are travelling the dark journey with us. Oh be swift to love, make haste to be kind." – Henri Frederic Amiel (1821-1881)

150. "I should have no objection to go over the same life from its beginning to the end: requesting only the advantage authors have, of correcting in a second edition the faults of the first." – Benjamin Franklin (1706-1790)

151. "Even a broken clock is right twice a day." – Unknown Source

152. "Life, an age to the miserable, and a moment to the happy." – Francis Bacon (1561-1626)

153. "No bastard ever one a war by dying for his country. He won it by making the other poor dumb bastard die for his country." – George S. Patton (1885-1945)

154. "Better to fight for something then live for nothing." – George S. Patton (1885-1945)

155. "The quality of a person's life is in direct proportion to their commitment to excellence, regardless of their chosen field of endeavor." – Vince Lombardi (1913-1970)

156. "Love will find a way. Indifference will find an excuse." – Unknown Source

157. "I have decided to stick with love. Hate is too great a burden to bear." – Martin Luther King Jr. (1929-1968)

158. "And remember, my sentimental friend, that a heart is not judged by how much you love, but by how much you are loved by others." --The Wizard of Oz.

159. "Love the whole world as a mother loves her only child." – Buddha (563-483B.C.)

160. "I try to give to the poor people for love what the rich could get for money. No, I wouldn't touch a leper for a thousand pounds; yet I willingly cure him for the love of God." – Mother Teresa (1910-1997)

161. "The value of love will always be stronger than the value of hate. Any nation or group of nations which employs hatred eventually is torn to pieces by hatred." – Franklin D. Roosevelt (1882-1945)

162. "Love is like an hourglass, with the heart filling up as the brain empties." – Jules Renard (1864-1910)

163. "There is no more lovely, friendly, and charming relationship, communion, or company than a good marriage." – Martin Luther (1483-1546)

164. "A good marriage would be between a blind wife and a deaf husband." – Michel Eyquem de Montaigne (1533-1592)

165. "Money talks and often says, 'Good Bye'." – Unknown Source

166. "The lack of money is the root of all evils." – Mark Twain (1835-1910)

167. "When a man assumes a public trust he should consider himself a public property." – Thomas Jefferson (1743-1826)

168. "I am in politics because of the conflict between good and evil, and I believe that in the end good will triumph." – Margaret Thatcher

169. "Politicians should never put themselves first: governments should put people first and all of us should put our country first." – Unknown Source

170. "Politics is far more complicated than physics." – Albert Einstein (1879-1955)

171. "Politicians have the ability to foretell what is going to happen tomorrow, next week, next month and next year. And to have the ability afterward to explain why it didn't happen." – Winston Churchill (1874-1965)

172. "He who pays the piper calls the tune." – Proverb

173. "I have learned through bitter experience the one supreme lesson to conserve my anger, and as heat conserved is transmitted into energy, even so our anger controlled can be transmitted into a power that can move the world." – Mahatma Gandhi (1869-1948)

174. "I am only one, but still I am one. I cannot do everything, but still I can do something; and because I cannot do everything, I will not refuse to do something that I can do." – Helen Keller (1880-1968)

175. "Enemies are so stimulating." – Katharine Hepburn (1907-2003)

176. "Life is to be lived. If you have to support yourself, you had bloody well better find some way that is going to be interesting. And you don't do that by sitting around." – Katharine Hepburn (1907-2003)

177. "Trying to be fascinating is an asinine position to be in." – Katharine Hepburn (1907-2003)

178. "If the world was perfect, it wouldn't be." – Yogi Berra

179. "It ain't over till it's over." – Yogi Berra

180. "Be good to others, that will protect you against evil." – Abu Bakr (573-634)

181. "I see that the path of progress has never taken a straight line, but has always been a zigzag course amid the conflicting forces of right and wrong, truth and error, justice and injustice, cruelty and mercy." – Kelly Miller (1863-1939)

182. "Civilization began the first time an angry person cast a word instead of a rock." – Sigmund Freud (1856-1939)

183. "Whoever loves becomes humble. Those who love have, so to speak, pawned a part of their narcissism." – Sigmund Freud (1856-1939)

184. "Even though your kids will consistently do the exact opposite of what you're telling them to do, you have to keep loving them just as much." – Bill Cosby

185. "The promise given was a necessity of the past: the word broken is a necessity of the present." – Niccolo Machiavelli (1469-1527)

186. "In order to succeed, your desire for success should be greater than your fear of failure." – Bill Cosby

187. "The heart of marriage is memories; and if the two of you happen to have the same ones and can savor your reruns, then your marriage is a gift from the gods." – Bill Cosby

188. "It pays to know the enemy – not least because at some time you may have the opportunity to turn him into a friend." – Margaret Thatcher

189. "To me, consensus seems to be the process of abandoning all beliefs, principles, values and policies. So it is something in which no one believes and to which no one objects." – Margaret Thatcher

190. "You may have to fight a battle more than once to win it." – Margaret Thatcher

191. "I know in my heart that man is good. That what is right will always eventually triumph. And there's purpose and worth to each and every life." – Ronald Reagan (1911-2004)

192. "Change will not come if we wait for some other person or some other time. We are the ones we've been waiting for. We are the change that we seek." – Barack Obama

193. "Focusing your life solely on making a buck shows a certain poverty of ambition. It asks too little of yourself. Because it's only when you hitch your wagon to something larger than yourself that you realize your true potential." – Barack Obama

194. "It took a lot of blood, sweat and tears to get to where we are today, but we have just begun. Today we begin in earnest the work of making sure that the world we leave our children is just a little bit better than the one we inhabit today." – Barack Obama

195. "To find yourself, think for yourself." – Socrates (469-399B.C.)

196. "We are what we think. All that we are arises with our thoughts. With our thoughts, we make our world." – Buddha (563-483B.C.)

197. "It is easier to perceive error than to find truth, for the former lies on the surface and is easily seen, while the latter lies in the depth, where few are willing to search for it." – Johann Wolfgang Von Goethe (1749-1832)

198. "Life is what we make of it, always has been, always will be." – Grandma Moses (1860-1961)

199. "Politics should be the part-time profession of every citizen who would protect the rights and privileges of free people and who would preserve what is good and fruitful in our national heritage." – Lucille Ball (1911-1989)

200. "The strength of a nation derives from the integrity of the home." – Confucius (551-479B.C.)

201. "By working faithfully eight hours a day, you may eventually get to be a boss and work twelve hours a day." – Robert Frost (1875-1963)

202. "It is the working man who is the happy man. It is the idle man who is the miserable man." – Benjamin Franklin (1706-1790)

203. "Europe will never be like America. Europe is a product of history. America is a product of philosophy. – Margaret Thatcher

204. "All work and no play makes Jack a dull boy, and Jill a wealthy widow." – Unknown Source

205. "Most men would feel insulted if it were proposed to employ them in throwing stones over a wall, and then in throwing them back, merely that they might earn their wages. But many are no more worthily employed now." – Henry David Thoreau (1817-1862)

206. "The people to fear are not those who disagree with you, but those who disagree and are too cowardly to let you know." – Napoleon Bonaparte (1769-1821)

207. "Governing a great nation is like cooking a small fish – too much handling will spoil it." – Lao Tzu (6th century B.C.)

208. "Knowing others is wisdom, knowing yourself is Enlightenment." – Lao Tzu (6th century B.C.)

209. "I learned long ago, never to wrestle with a pig. You get dirty, and besides, the pig likes it." – George Bernard Shaw (1856-1950)
210. "With great power comes great responsibility." -- Stan Lee
211. "Nuff Said" – Stan Lee

REFERENCE

General Reference Sources
www.ask.com – definitions
www.about.com - reference
www.answers.com – definitions, biographies
www.dictionary.com – definitions
www.wisegeek.com - reference
www.proverbia.net – quotes
www.ascensiongateway.com – quotes
www.brainyquote.com – quotes
www.womenshistory.about.com – famous women's quotes
www.famousquotes.com – Prophet Muhammad quotes
www.usconstitution.net/declar.html - U.S. Constitution Online
www.fightingmaster.com/masters/brucelee/quotes.htm - Bruce Lee Quotes
www.aneki.com – economic and other world rankings
www.globalissues.org/article/26/poverty-facts-and-stats - Global poverty statistics
www.cia.gov/library/publications/the-world-factbook/rankorder/2102rank.html - Life Expectancy statistics
www.billofrights.org – US Bill of Rights www.archives.gov/exhibits/charters/constitution_amendments_11-27.html - Amendments 11-27 of the Bill of Rights
www.foundingfathers.info – Quotes of the founding fathers of the United States

References
Anitei, Stefan (2008) Softpedia. Dolphin Saves Stranded Whales in New Zealand. Retrieved 4/15/09 from http://news.softpedia.com/news/Dolphin-Saves-Standed-Whales-80817.shtml

Bohen, Robert (2009) Anti Aging Research Laboratories. Life Span and Life Expectancy. Theory of Life Span. Retrieved 4/10/09 from http://www.antiagingresearch.com/life_span.shtml

Gould, Stephen Jay (1996) The Tallest Tale. Retrieved 4/11/09 from http://www.whyevolution.com/giraffe.html

Gu, Wei (2009) When the invisible hand fails, try China's 'two hands. Retrieved 4/12/09 from http://www.forbes.com/feeds/afx/2009/02/25/afx6092702.html)

Hart, Eloise (1985) The Delphic Oracle. Retrieved 5/4/09 from http://www.theosophy-nw.org/theosnw/world/med/me-elo.htm

Jones, Do-While (2002) Evolutionists on the Verge of Extinction. Retrieved 4/11/09 from http://www.scienceagainstevolution.org/v6i9f.htm

King, Todd (2001) Dante's Inferno A virtual Tour of Hell. Retrieved 4/6/09 from http://web.eku.edu/flash/inferno/

Lindsay, Don (2009) A List of Fallacious Arguments. Retrieved 4/13/09 from http://www.don-lindsay-archive.org/skeptic/arguments.html

Paley, William (1809) Natural Theology: or, Evidences of the Existence and Attributes of the Deity. Retrieved 04/11/09 from http://www.godandscience.org/evolution/paley.html

Rosenberg, Matt. About.com: Geography. Eratosthenes. Retrieved 4/11/09 from http://geography.about.com/od/historyofgeography/a/eratosthenes.htm

Tzu, Sun (600B.C.) The Art of War. Translated by Lionel Giles, M.A. in 1910. Retrieved 4/10/09 from http://www.chinapage.com/sunzi-e.html

Staff, Evidence for God. What will hell be like? Retrieved 4/5/09 from http://www.godandscience.org/doctrine/hell.html

Staff (2002) Lawmakers blast Pledge ruling. Retrieved 5/23/09 from http://archives.cnn.com/2002/LAW/06/26/pledge.allegiance

Staff (2008) Egyptology Online. Alexandria. Retrieved 4/5/09 from http://www.egyptologyonline.com/alexandria.htm

Staff (2007) Near-Death Experiences and the Afterlife. Scientific Evidence for Survival of Consciousness after Death. Retrieved 4/6/09 from http://www.near-death.com/evidence.html

Staff. University of California Museum of Paleontology. Understanding Evolution. Retrieved 04/11/09 from http://evolution.berkeley.edu/evolibrary/home.php

Staff. All About Creation. How Old is the Earth? Natural chronometers. Retrieved 4/11/09 from http://www.allaboutcreation.org/how-old-is-the-earth.htm

Staff (1998) Chipper Woods Bird Observatory. Brown-headed Cowbird. Retrieved 4/15/09 from http://www.wbu.com/chipperwoods/photos/cowbird.htm

Staff (2008) Defining Critical Thinking. Why Critical Thinking? Retrieved 04/13/09 from http://www.criticalthinking.org/aboutCT/definingCT.cfm

Staff. Answers in Creation. Old Earth Belief. Retrieved 04/16/09 from http://www.answersincreation.org/old.htm

Staff, Temple Apollo. About Apollon. Retrieved 05/03/09 from http://www.templeapollo.com/apollon.html

Stassen, Chris (2005) The Age of the Earth. Retrieved 04/11/09 from http://www.talkorigins.org/faqs/faq-age-of-earth.html

Van Wagner, Kendra. About.com: Psychology. The Milgram Obedience Experiment. Retrieved 06/11/09 from http://psychology.about.com/od/historyofpsychology/a/milgram.htm

Van Wyhe, John (2002) Charles Darwin: Gentleman Naturalist. Retrieved 04/11/09 from http://darwin-online.org.uk/darwin.html